YOU
GOT THE PART!

**A CASTING DIRECTOR
GUIDES ACTORS TO
SUCCESSFUL AUDITIONS
FOR FILM AND TV**

marsha chesley

Cover and interior design by Suzanne Braun/ Relish Design Studios Ltd.

We acknowledge the financial support of the Manitoba Arts Council, The Canada Council for the Arts and the Government of Canada through the Book Publishing Industry Development Program (BPIDP) for our publishing program.

Printed and bound in Canada

National Library of Canada Cataloguing in Publication

Chesley, Marsha
     You got the part!: a casting director guides actors to successful auditions for film and TV/Marsha Chesley.

Includes bibliographical references.
ISBN 0-920486-71-1

     1. Acting-Auditions. I. Title.

PN2071.A92C43 2004   792.02'8   C2004-902564-3

J. Gordon Shillingford Publishing Inc.
P.O. Box 86, RPO Corydon Avenue, Winnipeg, MB R3M 3S3

This book is dedicated to my best productions—
Rebecca and Aaron

And it's also for the Boy in the Backyard.

ACKNOWLEDGEMENTS

would like to thank all my "friendly readers" who gave me their comments and their encouragement: Rachel Carthew, Sean Carthew, Wendy Dennis, Ben Gordon, Jennifer Dean, Raymond Storey, Jimmy Simon, Bena Shuster, Linda Goranson, Gale Zoë Garnett and Eric Peterson.

I owe special thanks to Shari Caldwell and Alicia Jeffery of Caldwell Jeffery for their constant support and their insight into the work of agents. Heather Sangster showed me how to keep it clean and consistent. Tony Duarte's advice helped make it possible. David Barlow has always been a mentor and a friend. Martin Wiener went beyond the call of friendship by reviewing the manuscript three times. His comments were, as always, impeccable and invaluable.

There is no doubt that I would not have had the courage to attempt the writing of this book without the help and encouragement of Beth Kaplan. She is an extraordinary teacher. She was patient and helpful and always right. And a big hug to Debbie, Gillian, Gerry, Kerry, Jess and Sylvia—for listening.

Without Leonard McHardy and John Harvey of TheatreBooks the manuscript would not have found its way to Gordon Shillingford. I thank them for all their efforts on my behalf and I thank Gordon for having enough faith in this book to publish it.

Finally, I want to thank all the actors who have ever auditioned for me. They are my inspiration. And to those who shared their stories and anecdotes, I hope I have done them justice.

CONTENTS

Casting Myths Key   1
Prologue   3
Introduction   7

CHAPTER 1   The Invisible Profession   11
             Casting Without Auditions: Leading Roles
               or Cameos   15
             Casting the Usual Way—With Auditions   16

CHAPTER 2   Accomplishing the Impossible   21
             Getting an Agent   24
             Working with Your Agent   27
             What's in a Photograph?   30
             Being Pushy   32

CHAPTER 3   Preparation "A"—The Day Before   35
             The "Sides"   37
             "Boldly Go"   39
             Beating Back Boredom   41
             Black Tie and Tails or Jeans and a T?   43
             A Little Something Extra   45

CHAPTER 4   Preparation "B"—Building on the Text   47
             One-Liners   49
             Real "Scenes"   52

CHAPTER 5   Final Preparation Top Ten List   61

CHAPTER 6   Show Time   71
             The Etiquette of the Room   73
             The Execution   75
             Directors   81
             Chutzpah   86
             The Departure   88

CHAPTER 7   When the Lights Are Turned Off, What Goes On?   89

CHAPTER 8   Demo Reels, Self-Made Tapes, and Callbacks   97

CHAPTER 9   Debriefing and Keeping in Touch   107

CHAPTER 10 Staying Busy When You're Not   115

EPILOGUE   Audition Stories   123

MARSHA CHESLEY

Over the years I have heard of many *myths* about the casting process and about auditioning. I know that actors believe most of them so I will try to disprove the following *myths* in this book.

#1:   Casting directors don't want you to do well. (Intro)

#2:   Casting directors are always working, and if I have not called you in to audition in a long time it's because I have suddenly decided that you can't act and should get out of the business and find a new career. (Ch. 1)

#3:   Anyone can be an actor; desire is all you need. (Ch. 2)

#4:   When you are acting for the camera, don't be too big. You have to make everything smaller than you would on stage. (Ch. 3)

#5:   You don't have to do any preparation for a one-line part. (Ch. 4)

#6:   Your agent has already sent your picture and résumé ahead of time so you don't need to bring them with you to the audition. (Ch. 5)

#7:   Directors are really smart and well prepared and always know how to communicate to the actors exactly what they are looking for. (Ch. 6)

#8:   All casting decisions are obvious and clear and can be made easily. (Ch. 7)

#9:   The casting director makes all decisions about who should be cast in every role. (Ch. 7)

#10: "We both auditioned for the part. He got it, I didn't. Obviously he can act and I stink. I should quit now and give up this business altogether." (Ch. 7)

#11: "Don't call us, we'll call you." (Ch. 9)

#12: You can't work as an extra and expect to be called in to read for a speaking part. (Ch. 10)

I t was the early seventies, a time of touchy-feely interactive theatre. And there wasn't that much of it. In Toronto, where I grew up, Theatre Passe Muraille had started in 1967 emerging from the hippie culture of the day. Tarragon Theatre was next in 1970 with a mandate to develop and interpret new work. Then Toronto Free Theatre came along in 1971, specializing in "aggressive and transgressive theatre,"[1] whatever that meant. Anyone who wanted to could keep up with all the theatre there was to see in 1974. I was one of the ones who wanted to.

As a child I had done a lot of acting in school plays, drama festivals, and even some radio and semi-professional non-profit theatre. Not having the courage to pursue my dream, I became a high-school teacher—a high-school teacher who wanted to do something else. Afraid to quit my nice secure job, I started going to auditions for non-union plays. Non-union jobs rehearsed on evenings and weekends, so I thought I could continue to teach until I had established my acting career well enough to be able to quit.

An actor friend helped me choose a monologue for my audition piece. It came from *The Diary of Anne Frank*, a play I had acted in years before.[2] I even learned a song in case one was required. It was from *Godspell*. I was definitely of my generation.

I set out to get an audition and try my hand. There weren't very many, but I was determined to find them. I remember the feeling on audition days, the nerves that forced me to spend ages in the washroom and then several hours trying to look presentable. I did my best. I would fuss over my makeup and hair, striving for that perfectly casual effect. I would choose clothes to look my most alluring but also cool and carefree. Then, because of the times, I would often show up at the audition and be asked to do something ridiculous like get down on all fours and imitate every barnyard animal I could think of. No monologue, no song, just grunts and growls and crowing and clucking.

I would usually run into the same folks at these auditions. We would share stories, passing on word of other auditions, trying to encourage each other as much as possible. I was told that the usual callback rate was ten to one. If you got one callback for every ten auditions, you were doing well. I soon realized that my callback rate was much higher than that. Make no mistake: I was never cast, I just got called back a lot. But that was enough to keep me going. I was sure my day would come.

There was another convention I had yet to learn. At that time, there wasn't a network to get the word out about non-union auditions. So in order to have enough bodies show up, the people in charge would pass along the audition lists from one show to the organizers of another. Those people would call everyone on the list in the hopes of having enough auditioners show up so they would be able to cast their play. It had nothing whatsoever to do with the quality of the audition you had given. It had nothing to do with talent. It certainly had nothing to do with how appropriate you were for the part. They just needed living, breathing bodies. The first time I received one of those phone calls I was positive it was because I had been brilliant. I knew my Academy Award was just around the corner.

One day in midwinter, I got another of those phone calls, only this time the audition was for a play in Sudbury. When I hung up, I thought, "Sudbury? In February? I don't think so."

As I put down the phone I had an epiphany. I knew with absolute certainty that acting was not in my blood. If it's your passion, your bag is packed and ready. You will go anywhere, anytime, anyhow. You don't question that it's winter in Sudbury. You just go.

MARSHA CHESLEY

Of course, my belief in my talent did not waver. It was just the passion that was lacking. I never went to another audition. I immediately handed in a letter of resignation to my principal, finished out the year, and spent six months looking for a job in this business. Eventually I got hired in the very first casting department at CBC Television. That was in 1976, and I have been working in casting ever since. In all those years, the certainty of what I felt at the end of that phone call has endured. I have seen actors do whatever has been asked of them, whether it means travelling at the crack of dawn, spending months learning how to skate, swim, ride a horse or drive a motorcycle, being buried in sand or almost drowning for a role. They do it. Usually they do it joyously.

This is for all of them.

CHAPTER NOTES

1. The Toronto Free Theatre Web page.
2. I had played the lead, and my director was Lorne Lipowitz, who later became the icon of a generation as Lorne Michaels, the creator and executive producer of the long-running late night television show *Saturday Night Live.*

INTRODUCTION

Everyone knows that auditions are brutal. There's no other word for it. They are unnatural, awkward, stressful, and sometimes even unfair. But they have always been with us. As we saw in the movie *Shakespeare in Love*, even Will had to hold auditions. We can assume that further back, in the time of Aeschylus and Euripides, actors were sprucing up their togas to stand in torchlight and emote lines from the newest plays in hopes of snaring a role. No one has ever found a better way. So if auditions are still all we have, we had better make the best of them.

If you've ever auditioned for a role in a film or a television show and you didn't get it, this book is for you. If you've auditioned for lots of roles, didn't get them, and you wondered why, this book is for you. If you've trained for the stage but want to work in film, if you've done commercials or industrials or worked in any other media and want to try your hand at dramatic programming, this book is for you too. If you've ever directed or thought of directing, you will also find this book informative. And if you've ever wondered what really goes on in auditions, then read on.

In the following pages you'll find advice about how to get the audition and what to do with it once you have it. There are suggestions for properly preparing beforehand and following up later. And of course, there are the things I feel you should never do if you want to win the role. I should, perhaps, state that all these things are the gospel according to me—one individual casting director. If you speak to other casting directors, you will find certain differences in approach. But the basics won't change.

Auditions are a way for the decision-makers to get a sense of who is most right for the character in question, and get an indication of that actor's take on the part. We can even begin to sense what kind of person he[1] is. We get a chance to see what the actor looks like, hear what he sounds like, and determine if he is someone who will get along with the director. Can he take direction? How nervous is he and will he be able to calm those nerves and put them to good use? In callbacks we also look for chemistry: how does he match with the female lead or the other male leads he might have to interact with—a possible father or brother or buddy?

For the actor, his task in the audition is clear. He's there to prove that he's the best person for the job. He's there to shove the competition out of the way. He's there to prove that he's a brilliant actor so that even if he doesn't get this part, there might be something else for him either in this film or in the director's next project.

But it's also important to remember what auditions mean for the casting director. This is my showcase. This is where I get a chance to let the people who hired me know they've made the right decision and I'm sensational at my job. It's my opportunity to prove that I'm so in tune with the acting community, and I so understand the requirements of the roles, that I can provide the director with first-rate actors who are exactly what he's looking for. In fact, the best thing that can happen to me is that every person who comes in to audition is so perfect that we can't decide who to hire.

From time to time I'll try to dispel some common misconceptions such as: *Casting Myth #1: Casting directors don't want you to do well.* Think about it. If you fail, I look bad. The worse you are, the worse I look. Therefore the better you are, the better I look.

So believe me when I say I'm rooting for you. I don't want to be embarrassed any more than you do. If I call you in for an audition, you have to know I think you can do it. That's especially true since every director I have worked with starts our first meeting with the same proclamation, "I need really great actors for this film." I'm waiting for the day when a director says, "I don't need good actors. You can find me some crummy ones if you like." What you can take from this is that you have to be a "really great actor" if you're going to get the part and, furthermore, I already think you are.

My main focus in this book is to tell you what you can do to give yourself the edge over all those who want the same role as you. As a casting director, I can only pave the way by inviting you to the audition. Once you are inside the room, it's up to you to win the role. Quite simply, you have to be better than everyone else and you have to show that to the people watching your audition. In order to do that, you have to start by believing it yourself. Because if you don't believe it, no one else will.

CHAPTER NOTES

1. Both males and females who act are referred to as actors, and I do acknowledge that there are approximately equal numbers of both. For simplicity I have chosen to use the masculine gender when referring to actors in this book.

THE INVISIBLE PROFESSION

C asting is invisible, or at least it's supposed to be. No little girl at six years of age says, "Gee, when I grow up I want to be a casting director!"[1] Even within the acting community we are often not recognized. I have called some actors in to audition for me several times and they still don't know who I am. But that's okay. If you're nervous or focused on what you're doing, it's absolutely understandable that you aren't concentrating on who brings you into the room. Besides, it's my job to know who you are, not yours to know me.

I did, however, once find myself in a situation where being a little visible was a definite advantage. Like many casting directors, my office is in my home. One Sunday, just after midnight, I happened to discover that my main phone line was out of order. When I called telephone repair, I was told there would be a three-day wait for a technician. That was entirely unacceptable. Although I have three lines, this was my work line, and I just couldn't be without it. I frantically explained about my home office and asked if the operator could find a way to help me out. She asked my name. I told her. She paused. She then went into a long dissertation about how she was only working at the phone company temporarily and she really wanted to be an actor. She had started doing her research by getting a list of all the casting directors in the country and she recognized my name. She wondered if I would mind very much if she picked my brain and asked me some questions. It's 12:30 in the morning and the telephone repair operator is asking for acting tips!

I actually found myself staring at the receiver cradled in my hand as if it were an object from Mars. My reply was that I would be happy to answer her questions if she would have someone at my office to fix my phone by 10:00 the next morning. She assured me she would, I answered her questions, and my phone was fixed by 10:30.

Generally, the casting is good when it's most invisible. When it's seamless it doesn't elicit comment either about the casting director or the choice of actors. Only when it's bad do we notice that those brother-and-sister duos don't really look alike, or that the heroine can no longer pass for twenty-five. When the acting is good we, the audience, accept whatever is presented to us. In the very successful independent film *You Can Count On Me,* Laura Linney played the sister of Mark Ruffalo. She's the ultimate blonde WASP, and he looks every bit the Italian he is. But they were both outstanding in the parts, so the fact that they don't look like brother and sister was completely ignored.

That leads to the question, "What the heck does a casting director do?" Even the most experienced actors often have no idea, so I'll tell you.

The first thing I have to do is get myself hired.

Casting Myth #2: Casting directors are always working, and if I have not called you in to audition in a long time it's because I have decided that you can't act and should get out of the business and find a new career. The truth? I'm a freelancer just like you. I have to send out my résumé, make cold calls, and go to interviews. Sometimes I get the job and sometimes I don't. If I haven't called you for an audition, maybe the work I've been doing had nothing in your category, or maybe I haven't found any work myself. (Although I should admit that there have been occasions when I think an actor should get out of the business and find a new career.)

Okay. So I get myself hired. Now what?

Let's start with the casting of the lead.

CASTING WITHOUT AUDITIONS: LEADING ROLES OR CAMEOS

There are actors who have achieved a certain status. They are well known and never have to audition—Tom Cruise, Julia Roberts, Brad Pitt, Mike Myers, etc. There are other actors who shouldn't have to audition but sometimes do.

> A film called *AWAKENINGS* was being cast recently by a big casting director in Los Angeles. It starred among others, Robert De Niro. An actress was needed to play De Niro's mother, and De Niro had requested Shelley Winters. Someone—the casting director, the producers, the director—*insisted* that Winters come in and read for the part. She did—come in, that is. She sat down across from the casting director, resting a satchel on her ample lap. There was a moment of silence. She reached into the satchel, pulled out an Oscar, and placed it on the desk in front of her. She waited another moment, then reached into the satchel again, pulling out another Oscar, which she placed on the desk beside the first. There was a long pause this time. "Some people think I can act," Winters said. "Do you still want me to read for this part?"
>
> "No, Miss Winters," the casting director said.[2]

When actors get offered roles they have not auditioned for, they assume it's because the director has specifically requested them. Sometimes that's the case. Usually it's not. The process starts with the producer and the director giving the casting director all the information required to find the right actor for the role, such as the character's age and ethnic background, the amount of money available, the dates of the shoot, and any special characteristics or skills required. Then the casting director provides a list of potential actors that goes not only to all the producers and the director, but to the network or studio as well.

That list is derived from every possible source the casting director has at her[3] disposal, and it is never finished. Names will constantly be added and deleted until the role is cast.

The List. It becomes as sacred as a religious artifact. It will be circulated to the director and the creative producer, as well as to all the executive producers (there are usually many), the network if there is one, the executives in charge of production for the production company, and the distributors, who play a very large role in the decision, especially for features and movies-of-the-week. It's the distributors who know what sells and where they can sell it. In fact, the less experienced the producer and the director, the more influence the distributor has over the choice of stars. Finally, after many conference calls and meetings, all parties will agree on the names that will remain on the list and the order in which they will appear. The casting director will then contact the agent of the first choice on the list. If the first choice is not available, I'll move on to the second choice, and so on, until I can make an offer. At that point I'll negotiate terms suitable to both parties. On occasion I can't make a deal, so I'll move on to the next name. Eventually, we have our lead locked in and we've done all this without the benefit of auditions.

I don't mean to suggest that we never audition the leads in films. Auditions are always the most common casting tool, but if there is a lead or a cameo where the people being considered are so well known that auditions are not required, this is the process we follow.

However, it's the rest of the casting we want to concern ourselves with in this book.

That's the part we all know about: getting the auditions and surviving them.

CASTING THE USUAL WAY—WITH AUDITIONS

After reading the script and making my own determinations about the roles, I meet with the producer and the director and get their notes. They give me any information that might not be apparent in the script but will help in the casting. They can tell me to ignore all the ages and descriptions or they can say that the ages in the script must be strictly adhered to. They can give me more information on the characters and even some history or back story if necessary. They also give me the names of actors they have in mind and would like to see, as well as actors they dislike and will never have in a film in their lifetime. With all this information in hand, I start to make my master lists for each role.

As I did for parts cast with no audition, I use whatever tools I have at my disposal. I will look at all the theatre programs of plays I've been to recently; I will refer to lists of the actors I have interviewed; I will think back to all the films I've seen and television I've watched and look at any notes I made; I will go through all of the agents' roster lists; I will talk to colleagues who may have cast something recently that had similar requirements. I will even refer to lists I made for previous shows that might be relevant for this one. And now with the Internet I have an additional tool. I can perform a search of the on-line databases that I use the most. That means if I'm looking for a person from a difficult ethnic background with an ability to speak a foreign language who is a specific age, I can list what I'm looking for and a search of the database will give me a list of those actors registered who have all the required characteristics or skills. Obviously not every actor in the country is on that database, but it's a good starting point.

There is, however, one *major* resource the casting director has: the agent. At the same time as I start making lists for a new project, I will be preparing a breakdown of the script in which I write a short synopsis of the plot and a brief description of each character. That breakdown is disseminated to every agent in the country. It used to be sent by fax overnight. Now most casting directors send it on-line, so my breakdown is received by each agent in a matter of seconds, and they can start to respond with their suggestions immediately.

This is the agents' opportunity to be creative. They will give me suggestions from the actors on their rosters whom they think I should call in to audition. Sometimes an agent will add notes to try to "push" me to see someone who might not be instantly obvious for the part. Often he will call me to insist. Maybe he has more information about the actor that would make him a more attractive candidate. Maybe the actor did a performance out of town that I didn't see but was very similar to the one I'm looking for. Maybe he knows that the actor is more versatile than I might realize. Or maybe the agent is way off base and I ignore his suggestions completely.

Let me give you a sense of what I'm dealing with. When the breakdown used to go out by fax, I would receive hard copies of all the agents' suggestions within twenty-four hours. Big plastic bags of photos and résumés were delivered to me from all the agencies in town. If I were to stack those packages on top of each other, they would usually reach a height of three feet or more for a typical movie-of-the-week or feature film. And that would just be the suggestions from the agents in town. Then over the next few days packages would arrive from other cities across the country. The number of suggestions from agents would reach into the thousands.

Now that it's almost all done on-line, it saves a lot of paper but doesn't diminish the number of suggestions. In fact, it's just the opposite. The professional casting Web site I use tells me how many actors have been suggested for each character. It's usually 125 to 200 submissions per role. However, when I have put out a breakdown for continuing leads in a series, I have sometimes had more than 500 submissions for each one. Such is the competition. I go through every photo and résumé and build my master list for each role. Anyone who might be a possibility goes on that list. When the lists are all complete, I'll start to put together a casting session. If there's time, I will sometimes pre-screen actors I don't know. If not, I'll call in my first five or six choices for each role to audition for me, the producer, and the director. That means that I'll call in the ones I think are most likely to be what the director is looking for, and who I think can handle the acting requirements.

So the actor's name must first find its way onto my master list. Then it has to be in the first group I want to see. Obviously, if we don't cast someone from the first five or six auditions, we'll keep seeing more actors, five or six at a time. Hopefully we won't run out of time until we've made our selection. Sometimes we need to see 25 actors before we cast a role or maybe 200—whatever it takes. Occasionally we find the right actor immediately and we never see any more than the first six who came in on day one.

With series television, there is not the same luxury of time. I am usually given half a day with the director to cast a whole episode. So depending on the size of the cast, I can't bring in very many actors per role—sometimes as few as three or four. That means I have to get it right the first time.

So, the question is: How do you get on my master list and then how do you get to the top of it?

CHAPTER NOTES

1. A little aside—we are casting directors, not casting agents. It's a common mistake and one we go to great pains to correct. Agents represent actors and try to get them work. Casting directors hire actors. So there is no such thing as a casting agent.

2. Trish Deitch Rohrer, *Premier Magazine*, February 1990. Casting directors know the talent. Audition requests usually come from producers or directors.

3. We could discuss why the majority of casting directors are female. I don't know the answer, but I mention it here only as an explanation for why I have referred to the casting director as "her."

accomplishing the impossible

CHAPTER TWO

ACCOMPLISHING
THE IMPOSSIBLE

et's start from the beginning. I can't put you on my list if I
don't know who you are. So your first real task is finding a
way for me to become familiar with your work. How can
you do that? Years ago it used to be possible to be an actor and
have a decent career without having an agent. Today it isn't. The
industry has become too big and complex. If you did hear about
an audition independently, it would probably be over by the time
you found out where it was taking place. And just so there is no
misunderstanding—crashing auditions is just not done—*ever*. If
there's an open call then it's fair territory, but otherwise you will
just make people cross, they will fall behind if they have to take
time to deal with you, and they will only remember you as a pain
in the butt.

So I guess we really have to begin with getting an agent. An
actor's life isn't easy. Becoming an actor isn't easy either. This book
isn't intended as a primer on how to become an actor, but rather
what you can do as a professional actor to maximize your chances
of getting roles on film and television through the on-camera
audition process. Success presupposes a certain level of talent—as
well as training and experience.

Casting Myth #3: Anyone can be an actor; desire is all you need.
I'm here to tell you that just isn't so. If I want to be a brain
surgeon, I can't hang up a shingle and call myself a brain
surgeon. I need to study and go to school and spend years
preparing. It's the same for every profession or trade. Why do

people believe acting is different? Maybe it's because we've all heard the stories about someone being discovered just by breathing—like Lana Turner, who was spotted sitting in Schwab's Drug Store in Hollywood. Well, that was a million years ago, and for every story like that one, there are ten million others where actors are working hard and slugging it out trying to make it, sometimes successfully but usually not. As anyone who has made any efforts towards becoming an actor knows, it requires training and lots of hard work just like everything else. So if you've decided to walk in off the street and get an agent, you will be disappointed.

GETTING AN AGENT

I'll assume that you already have the training and are ready to call yourself a professional actor. So when you approach agents, make sure you do that professionally as well. Do your homework and only approach agents who are appropriate for you. Just as there are different types of actors, there are different types of agents. If you are not a union member, don't contact an agency that will only take union members. If you know that an agency has only very well-known and highly visible actors and you are just starting out, don't go there.

The first approach should be the good old-fashioned way—by mail. Most agents can't have their fax machines constantly busy receiving photos. It also uses up their ink. E-mail is very invasive and time-consuming. It's used so much for conducting daily business activities and after wading through all the "spam" it's impossible to handle anything more. And if there is any interest, it requires the further step of printing the pages.

The initial package you send to an agent when you're requesting representation should be carefully put together. Most agents want something that looks professional but not like you're trying too hard. Usually they require two different photographs, some recent reviews if you have them, one or two letters of recommendation, a professional résumé, and a short, catchy cover letter. Say how long you have been acting and a few words about your training. Anything more is an expensive waste of time and looks like overkill.

Send the package to the agent's office and wait at least ten days before you follow up with a phone call. While you're waiting for word, don't accost the agent if you happen to run into him at a play or elsewhere. And you'll really make him cross if you call him at home. Agents have a lot of work to do at home in the evenings representing the clients they already have. They really can't start talking to actors who aren't their clients when the time isn't appropriate.

If the agent does call you, even meets with you and the contact is favourable but he isn't able to take you on at that time, he may ask you to keep in touch. You can do that with a brief postcard from time to time, or mail notices of shows you are appearing in. Be careful about inviting an agent to see you in a production that isn't worth his time. If the evening isn't going to be enjoyable, the agent might not feel predisposed to taking you on. Remember that good agents spend a lot of time seeing their clients in productions of varying quality. Make sure you invite them for an evening that won't feel too much like work.

When you go out agent hunting, you'll also find that every agent will have different criteria for choosing whom they will represent. They have different needs in terms of filling their rosters. Obviously, first and foremost, they are looking for talent. But perhaps they don't have someone of a certain age, or they don't have a female comedian, or they don't have many people of colour. If that's the case, they will be looking for actors to fill in those gaps. They might not want to consider someone in an area where they are already well represented.

Agents will also have different methods of choosing potential clients and assessing their talent. Some will want to see you act in something, even if it's a school production. Some will have you do a cold reading. Some will want a prepared monologue. There are often showcases where agents are invited to see productions of the graduating students of theatre schools or acting classes. In some acting workshops the students will be given a videotape of the work they did over the course of the sessions. Some agents will want to see that tape. It would also help if you have a recommendation from someone the agent knows and respects—perhaps a director or another actor. All agents will want to see a résumé with something on it—both training and experience.

But even with a decent résumé it will often be difficult to entice an agent to take you on. If they say they don't want to duplicate actors they already represent, that means they have someone who is roughly the same age as you and of a similar type. They feel they can only really push one actor for a role, and if they have three or four who occupy the same niche then they would have to choose which one to push. They can't push all four and convince a potential engager that all are equally right for the part.

Actors who are just starting out tend to be in their late teens or early twenties. That's when most people begin their careers. If you are a recent graduate of a theatre school, you'll be competing with all the other recent graduates of all the theatre schools and acting classes and child performers who are now reaching adulthood. It's the area of greatest concentration. But the good news is that although the greatest competition is within the group of younger actors, people are always growing older. That means there is always room for new talent at the younger end.

If times are lean, that means there isn't much work around, so agents are having trouble getting enough work and auditions for the clients they already represent, and will not want to chance taking on any more. Some agents will only represent union members, and if you're just starting out chances are you are not yet in a union. Often it's a question of compatibility. If the agent feels that it just isn't a good fit, he won't take you on.

It's also worth noting that it's a big investment for an agent to take on a new client. Not only do agent and actor have to get to know each other, but the agent has to learn the actor's strengths and foibles, he has to learn just the right way to deal with the actor. He has to figure out what the actor is capable of and how to help him to grow and mature. But on the other side of the coin, the agent also has to make the world aware of that actor and what he is capable of. He has to build new résumés and make sure the photographs are good. He has to get demo reels made and out to the casting directors. He has to set up meetings and start making the actor's presence on his roster known by suggesting him appropriately for roles that come up. And the work the agent has to do for a new client is the same whether the person has lots of experience or none at all.

So getting taken on by the agent of your choice will be a tall order.

If you have all the necessary qualifications, you just have to keep on plugging. Keep phoning and sending out your résumés and taking meetings with anybody who will give you one and eventually you will be successful. But if you find that perhaps your qualifications are lacking, you may want to get some more training and try again at a later time.

WORKING WITH YOUR AGENT

Okay. So now you have an agent and you are thrilled to death with him. The next step is not to rely on him too much. Remember that you're a team. He should be working on your behalf, but you also have to get out there and do some things yourself.

When those breakdowns come out, you have to have faith that your agent knows you and your abilities well enough to suggest you for everything you are capable of doing. If you are just starting out and your agent has lofty ideals and only wants to send you out for large roles, you have to let him know that you are willing, (read that as "desperate") to take small roles as well (read that as "anything you can get"). And whether you have lots of experience or not, he should know if you're prepared to work for free on films being done by film-school students. You should be. After all, the students of today are going to be the brilliant directors of tomorrow. Also, because money is scarce and casts are small, the roles are usually plum—much better than you're likely to get on professional shoots when you're just starting out. Even auditioning for these freebies is good experience.

So your agent has suggested you, but this still doesn't help if I don't know you or your work. Your first response to that dilemma is to think that we actually have to meet, in person. Not so. If I can see your work, preferably on more than one occasion, I don't need to meet you to give you an audition. But if I haven't met you and I've never seen your work, several options are available to you. Encourage your agent to set up meetings with any of the casting directors you've not met. I often have what are called "go sees," where I interview actors at my office. I've also had agents set up an afternoon of interviews in their offices for me to see a few people I don't know. The difficulty is that when I'm busy with auditions, I don't usually have time to meet with actors who are not being seen for the project I'm working on. But don't give up. Eventually my calendar will clear again and I'll be able to schedule more "go sees." Not all casting directors will do them, but if they will it's worth pursuing.

If you're going to be in a play, a television show, or a film, you can contact me and let me know about it. As with contacting agents, "snail" mail is the best. You can also call and leave a short message. But better yet, get your agent to do it. I speak to so many agents all day long that your agent can mention your upcoming appearance to me when we are speaking about other business. I see as much theatre as I can and watch altogether too much television. I have three VCRs and there are many nights when all three are recording. I may not watch all of every show, but I do try to keep up with everything Canadian and also with most of the American shows made in Canada. So if I'm watching anyway, why not let me know to watch for you, even if you only have a few lines.

There is too much theatre around for me to see everything, but, although I'm pretty selective, I do go to a lot. It's another part of the job that I adore. I don't distinguish between the large theatres and the small—I go to both. I also try to hit the Fringe festivals and the Summerworks festivals, where I become familiar with new performers. Again, not all casting directors do this but it's still worthwhile letting them know you're in something. There's one other way to get me to see your work: a demo reel. (I'll talk more about demo reels and how to put them together, in Chapter 8.) If you haven't done much work, it's hard to put together a demo reel, so if you don't have enough material yet, don't worry about it. Eventually, you will. Don't misunderstand: A demo reel will rarely get an actor a role. What it will do is get your work seen by people who have not had the opportunity to see it first-hand. A demo should only include professional work—no film school projects or self-made tapes.

Self-made tapes have a purpose, but they shouldn't be used to show casting directors or producers or directors what you can do. The value of self-made tapes or school shows is educational. All the people involved are learning their craft and therefore these projects don't allow for the best judgment of your work. Those tapes can be used, however, to show prospective agents.

If you hear about a project and really feel that this is the one for you and you can't let it pass you by, you can tell your agent to give me some specific information that I might not have and that would encourage me to bring you in to audition. Maybe the part requires the actor to speak a language that you speak, or use a dialect that you can do to perfection. Maybe the director is someone you have worked with before. Maybe the agent has some press where you got good reviews for something similar and could forward them to me. These are effective mechanisms for making me see you, especially if it's for a role that is difficult to fill. But don't do this every time or it will lose its effectiveness.

One caveat: You better not lie. If you call up to beg for an audition and are granted one based on the fact that you say you can speak Spanish, then you really better be able to speak Spanish. How embarrassing for both of us if I believe you, call you in to read, and the director starts to chat with you in Spanish and you just sit there with your tongue hanging out. How many more times do you think I'll call you to audition?

One more word about agents: It's not a good idea to "dis" your agent. If you are at an audition, don't make any negative comments about your agent in any context. If you feel your agent hasn't passed on a relevant piece of information, then talk to the agent. Don't say anything to the casting director. I really don't want to hear about the problems you have with your agent. In fact you shouldn't be making negative comments about anyone. If you only have negative things to say, don't say anything at all.

WHAT'S IN A PHOTOGRAPH?

I'm constantly asked what I look for in an actor's photograph. Should it be moody? Should it be in colour or black and white? Should it be vertical or horizontal? The important thing to remember is that the photo is just a reminder of the person and what he or she looks like. The biggest no-no is to have a photo that doesn't resemble you at all. More women are guilty of this than men. Sometimes a woman gets hair and makeup done for a photo shoot that make her look like she has never looked before that day and never will again. Maybe she is presenting herself as she wishes she looked instead of how she does look. If I were to call you in based on the photo and get someone unrecognizable instead, it would make me cross. It registers at the same level as lying about speaking Spanish. For my purposes I don't even like photos filled with artsy poses and mood lighting. I just want to see an actual replica of the person who's in front of me.

It's also noteworthy that now that photos are so often posted on-line, vertical is more practical than horizontal. A full body shot is much less useful than a head shot. The first view that comes up on the computer screen is called a thumbnail. That thumbnail is only an inch high, so it needs to show the face and not a moody silhouette against a dark background. I can click on it to bring up a bigger view, but if I'm in a hurry I will probably skip right over one I can't see clearly. Remember that you want to give yourself every advantage, so if the casting director can't clearly identify you—at first glance—from your photograph, then you start out further back in the pack. Colour does stand out, but it's much more expensive. If the photo is good, you don't need to spend the extra money for colour unless you want to.

And, please, if your photo is from another decade, throw it out. I really don't care what you looked like when you were twenty pounds thinner or used to have hair.

Your résumé should be straightforward and easy to read. In the business world, there is a new trend to state your future goals and your motivation and personality traits. This is not required on an acting résumé. You want to list your credits in chronological order (starting with the most recent), your skills, and your training. You can also include any awards you may have received. Once you have hundreds of credits you'll want to pare them down so they'll fit on no more than two sides of a page. We don't need to know every one-liner you did thirty years ago. But when you are just starting out, your goal is to fill one page. At the beginning, your training will probably outweigh your credits, but that's okay. As the number of credits increases, you can remove some of the workshops you have attended but always keep some mention of your training and experience. The same thing can be said of commercials and extra work. You will be tempted to list all your commercials and every film where you appeared in the background, until you get enough other credits. And that is the right thing to do. As you get more speaking parts, you can reduce the number of extras you list. I'll talk further in Chapter 10 about why listing some credits as an extra can be beneficial, but in the meantime, you want the page to appear full and complete and make you look well rounded and experienced.

Again, I must caution you against lying. I have been given résumés where someone has listed a film I cast as one of their credits. But I never cast that actor in the film. I don't think it's a complete fabrication. The actor was probably an extra and he just embellished a little to make his résumé look better. But it sure gives me pause. I don't recommend doing that.

One last thought on photos and résumés: The photo should be stapled or glued back to back with the résumé. Why do so many people come in with them unstapled? Paper clips are not good enough. The picture always gets separated from the photo and it's very frustrating. Furthermore, if the actor's name isn't on the photo, then I might not remember who it is.

As a rule, directors and producers want everything handed to them in order without any effort required on their part. You should always be thinking about making things as easy as possible for them. Every little advantage you can give yourself will help, so don't sabotage a good audition by ignoring the details. Come in with your résumé stapled or glued to the photo.

BEING PUSHY

If you've tried everything mentioned in this chapter and you still can't get that first elusive audition with me, here is one thing you should not do. Don't send your photo and résumé to the director or the producer and start calling to bug them. All they will do is forward the info on to me. Their feeling is, "We hired a casting director to deal with the actors, so let her deal with the actors." Even if there is some tenuous connection—like you are a second cousin twice removed of the director's cleaning lady—there is still no point in writing because he will not read your covering letter long enough to find out. He will simply pass the whole thing on to me. If you really are a close friend of the director's, then he has probably already given me your name and asked that you be scheduled for an audition if, in fact, he thinks you are right for the part.

You have to be judicious about being pushy. If it's done too often, it can lose its effectiveness. And it can backfire. If you push too hard or too vehemently, it can make you look slightly crazy. Having said that, being pushy can sometimes be successful.

When I was casting an episode of a television series, time was short, as it always is in episodics. I'm usually given a maximum of half a day with the director to cast the whole thing. In this instance, an agent urged me to see her client for a small but important role. At this point, the auditions were the next day and all my six slots were filled for that role, with actors I was confident were right for it. I didn't have any room to squeeze in another actor, especially one I didn't know. The agent persisted, but I wouldn't budge. She called one last time to tell me that she felt so strongly that her client was right for this part that she had actually lined up a studio and the actor was going to pay to put herself on tape doing the audition. Then they would get the tape to me in time for us to consider it with the other six actors who were coming in to audition in person. At that point, I felt badly. I didn't want a struggling actor to have to spend a large sum of money if it was avoidable. Because I trusted this agent, I asked if the actor could come to my office that evening, after business hours, which was the only time I could see her, and I would pre-screen her. She came and she was terrific. I did work with her a little bit, but she was right on the money. So I squeezed her in for the next morning's casting session. If an agent does that and the person is wrong for the role or really can't deliver the goods, the agent's credibility with me would suffer and you can be sure I would not do that again. Even though this actress was up against some heavy hitters, she got the part.

I love it when that happens.

preparation "A" the day before

CHAPTER THREE

PREPARATION "A" –
THE DAY BEFORE

t's eleven-thirty in the morning. You're sitting at Second Cup drinking your second latte and reading the Entertainment section of the newspaper when your cellphone rings. It's your agent, who tells you he's managed to get you an important audition for the next day. He's got you other auditions before, but you haven't landed a role. This is it, your chance to prove that you can do it. All those months your agent has worked for you and you haven't earned a cent for him. After all, 15 per cent of zero is zero. He's done his part. So how can you maximize your chances for success this time?

THE "SIDES"

You have to start by getting the sides.[1] Usually, the agent will fax the sides to the actor, but if you don't have a fax machine or access to one, it's your responsibility to go to your agent's office and pick them up. At this point it's not usually necessary to read the whole script. Of course if you can, you give yourself an advantage, a big advantage. So if you're going to your agent's office anyway, you should take the time to look at the whole script if they have it. They usually have the script for films but probably won't for episodics because of the shortness of time.

Most agents will send a copy of my breakdown along with the sides. Make sure you read it. As long as you ignore the age and physical descriptions, all the rest of the information will help you.

Ignore the physical descriptions because if I've called you in, it's because I think you're right for it. However, if it really feels like a big mistake, have your agent check it out.

You need the synopsis of the story, but reading the descriptions of the other characters, not just your own, will enlighten you about the other people in your scene. If something on the page has been crossed out, it means it will not be read at the audition. Usually that's because there's too much dialogue belonging to other characters. We want to hear and see you, not the person reading with you. But make sure you read all the stuff that has an X through it. There might be some little clue in there that you can use.

The first thing you should do with the sides is make sure you understand the words. If there's something you don't understand, now is the time to get a dictionary and look it up. You'd be amazed how often an actor will come in to the audition room and ask what a particular word means. What that tells me is that he didn't spend any time preparing for the audition. How can he make intelligent choices about how to play the scene if he doesn't understand it?

Rarely will you get more than twenty-four hours' notice for a first audition. When it comes to callbacks, you'll usually get more time, but for now twenty-four hours will have to do. And this is where the real hard work takes place.

As you already know if you have auditioned before, when you're preparing a scene for an audition it's just like the work you do in scene-study class. I deal with the actual text in Chapter 4, but for every audition this is when you have to answer a lot of questions for yourself, such as: What is this scene about? What happens in this scene? How am I feeling? What do I want? What am I doing to get it? What do I think of the other people in this scene? Is there a change in the way I feel by the end of the scene? One way to check if you've answered the questions well enough is to try to keep going beyond the end of the scene. See if you can ad lib a continuation and be true to the character choices you've made. If you can't, you need to do some more work.

Perhaps the most important thing you have to resolve is: Why is this scene in the film? What function does it serve? Is it there just to give the audience some information? Is it there for comic purposes? Is it necessary for the development of character or plot? Only when you know that will you be able to make a choice as to how to approach the material.

A few years ago a well-known theatre actor and director asked me about taking my audition workshop. I was in awe of this actor and asked him why on earth he would want to do that. After all, he worked constantly on stage and was considered one of our leading theatre performers. He answered that although he did work frequently on stage, he had been going to film and television auditions lately and wasn't landing the roles. He wanted to try to find out why. He attended the weekend workshop and after twelve concentrated hours of doing auditions on camera and dissecting them with the rest of the participants, he came to me and was quite overwhelmed. He said that he had previously never done any preparation for film and television auditions. He would read the scene over a few times and just rely on his talent to carry him through. He was actually shocked at the amount of work required to make the audition powerful and successful. Looking back, he felt rather embarrassed about how he must have presented himself at those earlier auditions. His conclusion was that if he didn't have enough time to adequately prepare, it would be better not to go at all. A better idea is to find the time to prepare. It's your job.

"BOLDLY GO"

Casting Myth #4: When you are acting for the camera, don't be too big. You have to make everything smaller than you would on stage. Technically, this is true. The camera can see behind your eyes, so one of the most effective tools an actor can use on film is stillness. On stage, gestures have to be larger, the voice has to project to the last row, and even makeup has to be more exaggerated. So while the camera will pick up subtleties that might not be visible on stage, the one thing that must be big and bold is your choice.

When you come in to audition, you will likely be given no more than five minutes to make your brilliance known. There's no time for introduction or character development; you have to hit the ground running. From the instant the camera is turned on, we have to know who your character is. We have to know what you're thinking and feeling. If you're angry, we have to see it. If you're sad, we have to feel it. If you're happy, we should sense your joy. The worst thing you can do is make us guess what you were trying to get across and what emotions you were playing. If we can't see what you were trying for, then your choice hasn't been dynamic enough, it hasn't been big enough. So the day before, as you prepare for the audition, make sure you are going far enough, pushing hard enough, being bold enough to show us what you want us to see, but without using big gestures and facial expressions.

Making strong, clear choices is scary, especially when you have to do this without big physical gestures. Very often when you receive sides, and don't have access to the whole script, you have to make choices without having all the information at your disposal. That's all right. Everyone knows that you didn't have the whole script. What we want to see is what you can do with what you do have. If you need a piece of information and you don't have it, don't be afraid to make it up. If your choice is bold and clear and wrong, it's much better than trying to play it safe and ending up being wishy-washy.

For example, let's say you have a scene in which you are telling your girlfriend you are in love with her. You've chosen to play it with energy and effervescence. You're perky and happy and excited about all these challenges you're going to face. You may not know that two scenes before this one, your dog died. Obviously if you had known, you would have chosen to play the scene differently. But it doesn't matter. If your choice was carefully observed, we'll see it and note that you did it very well. Then the director will give you the information you didn't have and ask you to make the appropriate adjustment. That is infinitely better than playing the scene in such a way that no one can tell if you're happy or sad or irritated or creepy. So, big isn't always a bad thing.

This also brings up the need to stay flexible. Try it different ways at home, even after you've made your choice. If the director throws a curve ball at you, you need to be able to go with it.

Once you've decided on your approach to the scene, you have to memorize the material. *Always memorize.* The producers and the director appreciate the effort and realize that you have spent time and taken the audition seriously. There are bound to be occasions when circumstances are such that you can't memorize. If that's the case, then say so. Simply state that your child was ill, or you had three auditions on the same day, or you were out of town and didn't receive the sides until two hours ago. Be as familiar as you can with the material and still work through the answers to the key questions. But be careful. If you have an excuse for not memorizing every time you come in, I'll wonder if your life is just too busy and maybe I shouldn't call you in any more.

BEATING BACK BOREDOM

In the building blocks of putting together a good audition, you have to do more than just make a bold choice and memorize your lines. You have to make sure that you aren't boring. Being boring is the worst sin of all—worse than being bad. If you're really bad, you'll be remembered. If you're boring, you might just as well not have shown up.

So as you prepare, you should also be plotting your delivery. Approach every audition with all the training and experience you have. Preparing for an audition is just like rehearsing a scene in a play. You have to identify the places in the scene where you can inject some variety into your performance. Look for opportunities to speak more slowly or more quickly, to find room for a pause. Seek out a place to raise your voice or whisper if it will work in the scene. *Don't do these things just to show you can,* but seize every opportunity within the scene to avoid sameness. Also remember that you're trying to differentiate yourself from the other actors who will be reading for the same part. If you can find an unusual but sensible delivery, and do it well, you will surely be remembered at the end of the day.

These things all have to be plotted out based on the requirements of the scene and then written down in the margins of the page. Work out any physical business you may want to do and where you will want to stand or sit or lean forward or back. Plan it all and then memorize it along with the dialogue, so you'll be able to sustain the continuity in each take. Know it so well that you internalize it, then throw it away. You don't want it to look too studied. It's a lot of work, but remember that the more work you do the day before, the better you'll feel about the audition the day after.

Once you've done all that planning and plotting and memorizing, you have to try it out. That means that you have to do it—*out loud*. It's not good enough to go over and over it in your head. You have to hear it, and that means saying it out loud. For so many of us, when we hear music in our heads, we think we can reproduce it beautifully. Only when we open our mouths do we realize that we were not meant to be touring with an opera company or a rock band. It's the same with hearing the scene in your head. It's moving and funny and interesting. But say it out loud to make sure it's coming out the way you intended.

One of the riskiest things to do for an audition is to assume a dialect or accent that is not your own. Most actors think they can do them very well, when in reality they sound phony or pretentious or just plain bad. For television and film, we want you to be as close to yourself as possible. If I want a Scotsman or an Irishman or a Texan, I'll hire one. If I ask you to come in to audition, it's because I want you as you are. So if you've chosen to do a dialect that isn't your own and if you prepare by saying your lines out loud the day before, hopefully you'll be able to hear when you've made the wrong choice.[2] (All the same, I must point out that all Canadian actors should be able to sound American when required. A common criticism from American directors is, "He sounds too Canadian.")

When I was casting a television police series, one of the actors who played a guest-starring role told me about his experience doing his lines out loud the night before his audition. He was rehearsing at home in the apartment he'd lived in for many years and where he knew all his neighbours and they knew he was an actor. The scene he had to do for the audition required him to get very worked up and shout out the lines, "I didn't kill her! I loved her. I didn't kill anyone." He was apparently very convincing, because one of his neighbours, fearing the worst, called the police. When they came to investigate, he had to show them a copy of the sides as well as his picture and résumé to prove that he was an actor and was preparing for an audition. They eventually believed him, but not before a thorough search of his apartment. In the end, they were satisfied because one of the cops had gone to high school with the lead actress in our series. For some reason the police found that reassuring.

BLACK TIE AND TAILS OR JEANS AND A T?

I always get nervous when an actor pays too much attention to his wardrobe for an audition. While it's important to be comfortable and perhaps give an indication of the correct wardrobe for the role, you don't want to suggest that you're putting the role on from the outside, when it should be growing out from within. You're not being judged on your ability as a costume designer. You're being judged on your performance.

Do just enough preparation to help you feel right in the role. First of all, the obvious: If you're coming in to read for the role of a professional person, a lawyer or teacher, or businessman, don't wear ripped jeans and a dirty T-shirt. If you're coming in for a period piece, women can help themselves just by wearing a skirt. Both men and women will feel more like they're in another era simply by wearing a shirt that buttons up right to the neck. Most of us keep the top buttons open for comfort, but if you do up all the buttons your posture will improve. It's automatic. Try it. You'll see. You will sit or stand straighter. The bottom line is that you want to do enough to help with your performance and no more. Please don't go out and rent a policeman's uniform or a showgirl's tacky ensemble for an audition. It's overkill.

You can also help yourself in other ways. If you're coming in to read for a drug addict, you shouldn't have perfect hair and makeup. In fact, no makeup and dirty hair would be a better choice.

But do check out the clothes you intend to wear for your audition. Remember that stripes don't do well on video. Neither does too much solid black, white, or red. It's important to know that what you're wearing is comfortable, but it's more important to know if it will stand up to the test. An actress told me about an audition where she was reading for a heroin-addicted hooker. She wanted to look the part, so she put on a pair of ripped, frayed jeans. They were very old, very worn, very ripped, and also very tight. Because they were so tight she decided not to wear any underwear on the day. Everything was fine until the director asked her to sit down. Unfortunately she hadn't tried that at home and as she sat, she felt and heard the noise as the crotch of her jeans ripped from the navel right around to the top of her derrière. She finished the scene but not surprisingly her concentration lapsed. All she could think about was what to do when she was done. She held the sides in front of her until she was upright and then she placed them behind her as she walked out of the room. She said her cheeks were flapping in the breeze, but she had managed to keep her "womanly parts" covered. Not surprisingly, she didn't get the role.

Make sure you check out all your accessories as well. If a woman is wearing a very huge or brightly coloured pair of earrings, they can be distracting. In fact, it can have the same effect as spinach between your teeth—that's all anyone will look at. We will stop hearing the words and find ourselves focusing on the huge earrings or the spinach. Having a strand or two of long hair hanging down over the eyes is also distracting. I find myself brushing my own hair out of my face repeatedly while I'm watching the audition.

Hair can present several problems, especially if you're looking down. If your hair is long and loose, it can screen the eyes and be frustrating to watch. You should be prepared to clip or tie it back if it gets in the way of the camera seeing your face clearly.

The same advice about wardrobe can also apply to props. You're not being tested on your ability to be a props master. It's not a scavenger hunt. You don't need to find unusual objects to bring to the audition. Again, your goal is to give yourself an edge over everyone else. You have to feel confident and comfortable, so if there is one specific prop that will help you, then by all means, bring it along. If you're playing a detective you can bring a little notebook. If you want to carry a mug, then do. If you need a cellphone, then use one. *Just make sure it's turned off!* But you don't need to have these things. Remember, it's all about the performance. Use what will help you. Don't complicate things with wardrobe or props. Be sure they work for you, not against you.

A LITTLE SOMETHING EXTRA

Here's an audition tip I highly recommend and that is not often considered. Every time you're preparing for an audition you should also be preparing an answer to the question, "What have you been doing lately?" This has more significance than you might realize. Remember that the game is really all about making yourself look good and feel good. You are the one who'll feel bad if you can't think of an intelligent answer to that question. If you worked with a wonderful director and his name has slipped your mind, we won't give it two thoughts, but you will. You'll spend the next week flagellating yourself because you didn't remember that director's name. So get out your résumé, keep it up to date, and memorize the last few key things that might impress. And remember that it's important how you present yourself. If you have quite a number of recent credits, then it's easy to memorize and recite. But if your résumé is slim, it requires a bit of inventiveness—and by inventiveness I don't mean lying. Just be positive and creative.

I have a few scenarios. If the most recent credit you have is a two-line part on a television show, you could say, "Oh, I was on *Blue Murder,* but I only had two lines." Or you could give the same information this way: "I just did a scene on *Blue Murder.* I played opposite the lead and even though I only had a couple of lines, I had such a good time and I learned so much." Which one do you think makes a better impression?

Like most things, it's much more difficult to answer the question, "What have you been doing lately?" when you haven't been doing much. That's when you really have to be creative. Again, you shouldn't say, "Oh, I really haven't been doing much." You might try something like: "Well, things have been a little slow, so I've used this time to take some workshops, go to some theatre, and see some films I missed. I've also been reading a lot and getting together with friends to do some scene study. It's been very valuable." Don't blab on too long, but *keep it positive*.

Although the question is intended to find out about your recent acting work, you don't always have to answer that way. Anything that will make you memorable to the folks behind the table is a good thing. So if you just tried skydiving for the first time, or if you wrestled alligators in the Florida swamp, or if you went whale-watching off the coast of Newfoundland, you might want to mention it. We will remember. At the end of the day when we're recapping everyone we saw, someone will say, "You know, the blond, the guy who ran with the bulls in Pamplona." Anything you can do to assure that they will remember you is a good thing.

CHAPTER NOTES

1. Here's the story I was told about why "sides" are called sides. It seems that years ago each actor was given just his or her character's dialogue with only three to five cue words before each speech. So you received just one "side" of the conversation and, in fact, of the script. To save paper this was printed on half-size sheets. The custom hasn't entirely faded away though. It seems that Woody Allen still does it, but for "artistic" reasons, not to save paper.

2. There are always exceptions to any rule. Some people have superior talents for dialects. Think of Robin Williams. If you are one of those people, then by all means, use them when appropriate. Also if you lived in a country or have relatives from somewhere that has provided you with the means to learn a dialect or accent, then go for it. But don't fool yourself.

preparation "B"
building on the text

CHAPTER FOUR

PREPARATION "B" – BUILDING ON THE TEXT

ONE-LINERS

You're auditioning tomorrow for a small role in an episode of a television series. You've just received your sides. Here's what the scene looks like:

SC. 22   INT. RESTAURANT—DAY

> JAKE and SARAH are seated at a table at the back of the restaurant. A WAITRESS walks over to them.

> WAITRESS

> Hi there. What can I get for you folks today?

You are reading for the part of the waitress. Wow! What do you do with that? It seems so easy, you think anyone can say it.

Casting Myth #5: You don't have to do any preparation for a one-line part. Wrong. This is probably the most difficult audition you will ever face. Longer scenes have a beginning, a middle, and an end. Something happens. Relationships are evident. In a one-liner, you are given absolutely no information at all.

We've all seen those low-budget films where they try to save money by hiring a background performer (the person formerly known as an extra) who walks up to the table in the restaurant holding her notepad and pulling a pencil from behind her ear. She doesn't say a word because if she did, they would have to pay her a lot more money. It looks ridiculous and cheap and because it's unnatural it takes the audience right out of the scene even if they can't identify why. Clearly it's bad writing, and bad producing and directing for allowing this to happen. (Unfortunately an actor is often called upon to make something out of bad writing, but that, too, is his job.) In the above example the producer has wisely decided to spend the money, but that doesn't mean anyone has given the slightest thought to the person who will deliver the line.

Rest assured, not even the writer has thought about this waitress. Every line has to have a purpose. It should advance plot, reveal character, or establish mood. So a good writer will know why he included the line, but that doesn't mean he has given any thought to who the waitress should be. And you can be sure the director hasn't thought about her either, and he never will. On the day of the shoot he'll be busy dealing with a shadow falling over Jake's cheek or with a stray hair on Sarah's forehead or with a prop that doesn't suit the setting. In fact, the only time anyone will pay attention to this waitress is during the auditions. So it's up to you to decide who she is, because if you don't know, then we won't know either and you won't get the part. You should look at the rest of the scene, or as much of it as you were given, to try to figure out why the line was included. That will help you determine how to deliver it.

So who is she? Does she like her job? Is she bored? Is she keen? Is she desperate? Does she know Jake and Sarah? Does she like Jake and Sarah? Does she not like them? One thing that will help you create an identity for this waitress is to remember that for film auditions, you should always try to stick as closely as possible to who you are. That's especially true when the part is small. Use yourself. Don't try to make yourself into someone you are not. Also, think about the fact that your entire appearance on screen, should you get this role, will probably last for five seconds. The worst thing you can do is try to turn it into *King Lear*. You have to make it seem as natural as possible, so that means as little visible "acting" as possible.

It will also help you if you can figure out why the writer included the line.

You might decide that since this is a young waitress, she is new to the job and eager to please. So you could play her perky and energetic. You might think she hates this job and is just doing it for the money, so you play her with an edge. She might be desperate to keep this job because she's supporting her invalid mother and trying to put herself through school, so you play her nervous and fidgety. Or you could conceive of her as being as bored as can be, because she has been doing this so long she doesn't even see the customers any more. In that case, let us see the boredom.

If you're a perky, upbeat person, you should probably choose to play the perky, energetic waitress. If you tend to be a laid-back, world-weary kind of person, you should perhaps choose the bored approach. In five seconds, you'll get further by using yourself than by reaching for something else. So it makes good sense to know yourself and how you come across.

Unfortunately, I have met far too many actors who don't know themselves at all. For example, if you are a female who is naturally open and cute and vivacious, it will be much more difficult to be seen as a sultry vixen. If you know where you fit, you'll be much more likely to achieve success.

Next you have to decide what you think of the two people you are talking to. Decide if you like them or not, or if you are indifferent, or what. Then do all the rest of the work, plotting out how you will deliver the line and clearly showing us your choice. We should be able to determine everything you've worked out if you've really made the most of your five seconds. There is, however, one thing you might not be able to figure out. Look at every detail on the page for clues as to the type of restaurant this is. If it's a fairly upscale place, it will require a different waitress than if it's a seedy diner or a funky downtown bistro. If you can't find anything to tell you what kind of a place it is, make it up. Just make sure you know what it is in your own mind.

We've just spent almost three pages dissecting an audition of ten words! If you're ever in doubt about the old adage that there are no small parts, only small actors, then just think back to the movie *When Harry Met Sally*. Director Rob Reiner gave the most memorable line in that film to his mother. She was sitting in a restaurant overhearing Meg Ryan vividly illustrate how she can always fool men by "faking it." Mrs. Reiner brought down the house when she said, "I'll have what she's having!" And that's only five words!

REAL "SCENES"

When you have a larger scene—say three or four pages—read every single word on every page you are given, to find every clue. First, look at the heading for the scene. It's always surprising to me how many actors fail to take the relevant information from the scene heading, and it really can help you. It will look like this:

SC. 38 INT. COURTROOM—DAY."

Before you even look at the dialogue, you've learned quite a bit of information. First of all, this is Scene 38, so it's not the beginning of the film. If you also have the page number, you'll have a pretty good sense of where this scene fits into the whole piece. Next, you learn that the scene is an interior, so it's not competing with the outside elements. Obviously the courtroom location is indicative of what will be going on. And finally, you know that the scene takes place in the daytime. If that scene heading had been "SC. 2 EXT. LANE WAY—NIGHT," you would know that the approach you should be taking to this scene should be radically different from the previous one, and you still haven't read a single word of dialogue of either.

If the film has a number of flashbacks, the scene heading will also include the year: "SC. 38 INT. COURTROOM—DAY, 1964." How valuable to know what year you're supposed to be playing. Another example: In so many films that take place in big urban cities, we need reporters and journalists. If the audition piece is a media scrum, and the scene heading says, "SC. 57 EXT. CORONER'S COURT—DAY," you have to visualize where this scene will be shot. A media scrum means that there are lots of reporters fighting for position, forcing microphones in someone's face and competing for attention. The fact that the heading says it's an *exterior* means that the dialogue will also be competing with street and traffic noise—buses, streetcars, trucks, cars, pedestrians, planes, sirens, whistles, skateboards, and anything else that happens to be passing by. Before you've even looked at the words, you should have determined that you're going to have to shout, which you wouldn't have to do if this were an *interior*. In the audition, it's very hard to maintain the illusion of this busy street. But you have to. The auditioners will want to make sure that you are uninhibited enough to go for it—to shout out the lines and be heard over the crowd not in the audition room with you. Most actors fail to notice the heading, so they fail to shout out the lines. They also fail to get the part.

Let's look at the preparation for a specific scene. In the following, you will be auditioning for the role of Mrs. Clarke:

SC. 36 INT. POLICE STATION CORRIDOR—DAY

> MRS. CLARKE exits from inside a room followed by a police DETECTIVE. The detective puts a kindly hand on her shoulder.

DETECTIVE

Will you be all right, Mrs. Clarke?

MRS. CLARKE

Yes. Fine. Thank you, Detective.

DETECTIVE

I may have some more questions for you.
I'll call you a little later on.

MRS. CLARKE

Of course…

MRS. CLARKE

Oh, Detective, could I possibly make a phone call?

YOU GOT THE PART!

DETECTIVE

Sure.

He points to an office that opens onto the corridor.

DETECTIVE

There's my office. Just press nine.

MRS. CLARKE

Thank you.

DETECTIVE

Any time.

CUT TO:

SC. 37 INT. DETECTIVE'S OFFICE—DAY

Mrs. Clarke goes into the office and looks around. She goes over to the desk, lifts the receiver and makes a phone call.

MRS. CLARKE

Hi. It's me. No. Not yet. They asked me a lot of questions, but I can leave. I don't think so. I'm going there now. Okay. Bye.

CUT TO:

That's what you were given. Starting with the heading, you know this is Scenes 36 and 37, so you are more than a little way into the story. You know that this is daytime in a police station. Before you even read the dialogue, you should be thinking about what this location looks like. Visualize it. If you have ever walked into a police station in the middle of the day, you will know that they are busy places. So if the first of these two scenes takes place in the corridor, then you can assume that lots of people will be milling about. Maybe some will be seated on chairs. Phones will be ringing and fax machines will be clicking. There may even be some people yelling out cop to cop or perhaps to no one in particular.

You're reading for Mrs. Clarke. There is no age given for her, but don't let that bother you. She is your age. She is *Mrs.* Clarke so you know she is or was married. The detective has an office of his own, so he must be of fairly high rank. That would put him in plainclothes, not a uniform. The only other thing we know is that something happened and Mrs. Clarke is being interviewed about it. That leaves us with a whole lot of questions.

Who is Mrs. Clarke? What has happened? Is Mrs. Clarke involved? Does she know something? Does she know more than she has said? Does the detective believe her? What does she think of the detective? Has she been there a long time? Who does she call in the short second scene? Most important of all, is she guilty of something? Is she protecting someone? Is there a Mr. Clarke and if so, where is he? You can probably think of at least a dozen more questions to ask yourself here.

The answers you give to all those questions will determine how you play the scene. You will also have to decide if you want her to seem nervous. Most people, guilty or not, are nervous when they're questioned by police. You'll have to decide if she should seem upset or cool. Is she tired? You'll have to decide if she should be well dressed and crisp or rumpled. Or maybe she isn't well dressed at all. In other words, you have to know exactly who this woman is, what her state of mind is, and what she did or did not do. And make sure to check the breakdown you received with the sides for any possible answers to your questions. That might help.

After you've worked all that out, you have to begin to plot the delivery. Is there a spot where you can pause effectively? Will it all be played at the same voice level? Might she say some of the lines flirtatiously or would she be distracted and not really make eye contact?

It would be appropriate to play this scene standing because it takes place in the corridor. But you have to decide if you want to turn away before you ask to use the phone, and then turn back.

You could then walk out of frame and re-enter as if you are going into the office if you want, or you could just stay in one place. All these are choices for you, and you alone, to make.

With this scene, you've been given a gift that is not often available in audition pieces. You have a shift in location and a change in tone, which gives you the opportunity to show two different dimensions. You might show one side of the character in conversation with the detective and then show something else on the phone. The worst mistake you can make with this scene is to play both sections the same way. No matter what choices you make, you must see that two different attitudes are called for here, so you must show two different attitudes.

You should visualize the office just as you have the corridor, so you will know if there are glass walls that others can see through. Are you really alone in there? You will also know whether people in the corridor can hear your conversation. If you can be overheard, you will probably whisper or talk softly while you're on the phone. You might also be constantly on the lookout for the detective, who could suddenly reappear in his own office. So you should be thinking about your body language and what it will be saying. All of this should be plotted out as you prepare.

Most scenes don't give you two distinct pieces. Your task becomes more difficult if you have to try to create places to inject variety into your performance when the text seems to give you only one attitude.

Let's look at another scene. In this one, you are reading the part of Mike:

SC.14   EXT. AIRPORT RUNWAY—DAY

> Mike is at the airport out on a runway being interviewed by a newsman. He has a microphone in front of his face. There is a lot of activity behind him.

> MIKE[1]

> ..the seatbelt light came on and we knew we were just about to land. A few seconds later my

son starts pointing and shouting. I looked out
the window and saw this deer stopped on the
runway right in the path of the plane. It was just
staring straight ahead. It was too late for the
pilot to do anything. We slammed right into it.
God—it was awful.

First of all, place yourself in the location where you are being
interviewed, which is the airport runway. Visualize it.

Starting with the usual questions, figure out who Mike is.
Make a decision as to how you want Mike to appear, whether he
is distraught and hyper or maybe so upset that he is practically a
zombie. Decide how much time has elapsed since the incident
took place and how many times Mike has told the story.
Presumably the news crews got to the airport very quickly, but
why did they choose Mike to interview over all the other
passengers? Obviously you can start your preparation for any
scene with the same initial questions. But don't stop there. Each
situation has a different set of circumstances, so it requires a
different attack and there will always be some questions that don't
apply. But you will never run out of questions.

Let's decide that Mike is in shock and he's been standing at
the airport for a long time. Perhaps his son was crying and he took
him aside to try to calm him down. He has had to be strong for
his son, but by the time the television crew sticks that
microphone in his face, he is just exhausted and upset. He has not
told the story to anyone yet and is reliving the experience as he
expresses it. He is talking fairly slowly, as if in a daze. Try it
yourself. Say those lines right now out loud, slowly. There are lots
of natural pauses in that paragraph with a chance to do
something a little different for the last line, "God—it was awful."

If you did just read that paragraph out loud, I'll bet you
thought that you sounded boring. I don't want to suggest that
there is only one right way of delivering these lines, but I think
slow and in shock would be very hard to make interesting. It can
be done, but you really have to be creative. On the other hand, if
you choose to make Mike highly excitable and explosive, you will

allow yourself more room for variety in the delivery of the lines. The first three sentences could come out all in a rush, with barely any time for a breath. Then there are some good opportunities for pauses and a place to raise your voice, and finally a resolution that is a complete change from what you've done before. Let's look at it in detail.

Start off quickly and animated, looking at the interviewer:

> ...the seat belt light came on and we knew we were just about to land. A few seconds later my son starts pointing and shouting. I looked out the window and saw this deer stopped on the runway right in the path of the plane.

Pause.

Slow down your delivery for this next line. Look over at the runway.

> It was just staring straight ahead.

Pause.

Be excited again. Raise your voice.

> It was too late for the pilot to do anything. We slammed right into it.

Long pause.

Look away, as if you can't even bear the memory. Lower your voice to just above a whisper.

> God—it was awful.

Obviously, this is not the only way this scene could be played. But answering all the preparation questions and understanding your character are not enough if you can't make the delivery interesting. Sameness equals boring, and the last thing you want to be is boring. So you have to make sure that you don't read every line the same way. Find the nuances and the changes and surprise us. If you can find an interesting way to do the scene and you can deliver it well, you will be remembered at the end of the day.

MARSHA CHESLEY

Another thing that should be considered is that you often have to go further when you are auditioning than you will if you get the part and play the scene on camera. It's always much easier to pull a performance back than to push it further. The director will want to see in the audition that you have enough courage to go for it, to be as uninhibited as required. If you go a bit too far in any direction, he will ask you to pull it back and try again. But if you haven't gone far enough, he may think you are not able to. So don't be afraid to go for it.

You're finally ready to memorize the words and the delivery you have plotted for yourself. Then you should rehearse your gestures and looks and body language. Practise it enough times so that it doesn't seem memorized and studied. Make it as natural as possible so it will be as believable as possible. You don't ever want to look like you're "acting."

There is absolutely no doubt that the work you have just done is the most difficult part of your audition. Now you're ready for Show Time tomorrow. If you're well prepared, it should be a piece of cake.

CHAPTER NOTES

1. Both Mrs. Clarke and Mike are defined as *principal* roles while the Waitress in the earlier scene is an *actor* role. A principal role consists of six lines or more. Five lines or less is an actor role. A line of dialogue is defined as a complete sentence of ten words or less. For example, a sentence of twelve words is counted as two lines, whereas a sentence of three words is one line.

final preparation
top ten list

FINAL PREPARATION
TOP TEN LIST

This is my personal Top Ten List of the things you should do or should not do on the day of your audition, leading right up to the moment when you are called in to read.

1: REMAIN CALM.

Do whatever it takes, whatever works for you, to get your nerves under control. A little bit of nervousness is a good thing—it keeps you on your toes. But if you're incapacitated by nerves, it will certainly affect your performance. So go to the gym or for a walk or meditate to get control of it. It's not a good idea to spend every waking moment working on the piece. Keep things in perspective: this is not about life and death. You'll have other auditions to worry about in the future.

2: DON'T BE LATE.

Going to auditions is your job until you become a big star, so make sure you leave enough time to get there early. You should arrive at an audition at least twenty minutes before your scheduled time. The main reason for arriving early is to get yourself in the right headspace, but there are some practical reasons as well. It's possible that a new draft of the script has arrived since the sides were sent out and the director wants to hear the revised dialogue. So a new set of sides might be waiting for you at the audition. Also, there are those rare occasions when the auditions are actually *on time*. It's not a good idea to count on *them* running behind just so you won't have to wait.

Then, of course, there is the one occasion when you arrive nice and early to give yourself time to relax and get into the right frame of mind and they are actually running ahead of schedule. If they ask you to come in ten or fifteen minutes ahead of your appointment, you do have the right to say very nicely that you need a few more minutes to get ready. Don't feel obliged to go in early unless you want to. It's not your fault that someone didn't show up or that they didn't schedule their day very well. As long as it's before the time you were given, take as long as you want.

Let's talk about common courtesy for a moment. If you have a date with someone and you can't make it, you call and express your regrets. If you have an appointment and get sick, you call and cancel. If you're invited to someone's home for dinner and you're going to be late, you call ahead to alert the hostess. So if you have an audition and some unforeseen event happens and you just can't get there on time or at all, you should do everything you can to let the casting director know. You'd be amazed at how many times an actor just doesn't show up. That is rude on so many levels that we needn't bother to enumerate them. Things happen. It's Murphy's Law—anything that can go wrong will go wrong. So if you get into one of those spirals of disaster on audition day, just make sure you communicate with your agent. That's usually easier than finding out the phone number of the studio and trying to track down the casting director who's probably tied up in the auditions anyway. Your agent will know how to get a message to the appropriate place. It's extremely bad manners not to show up and certainly doesn't make someone want to invite you to the party next time.

3: DON'T GET PISSED OFF IF THE AUDITIONS ARE RUNNING LATE.

I really pride myself on keeping my auditions on time, but things happen. Maybe someone was given the wrong sides and we gave him some extra time to look at the right ones. Or maybe—and this is the most usual scenario—the producer or the director was late and we simply couldn't make up the time that was lost at the beginning of the day while we waited for the latecomer. Whatever the reason, it's pretty much the norm that auditions run ten or fifteen minutes behind schedule. So if your audition is at 2:00 p.m. you should plan to arrive no later than 1:40 and then be prepared not to be seen until 2:20.

If you're sitting in the waiting room fuming because the auditions are running late, you're the only one that will be affected. And if you're angry, you'll just wreck your audition and with it your chances of landing the role.

4: DON'T PARTY IN THE WAITING ROOM.

It's only logical that you'll see a lot of your friends at film and television auditions because, as I said earlier, we are going to cast people as closely as possible to themselves. So if we need a thirty-two-year-old schoolteacher, all the people I call in will be close to that age. If you've auditioned several times you will probably have noticed already that you see a lot of the same gang called in for the same roles as you. You may also know some of the actors who are auditioning for other roles. But resist every temptation to catch up on recent life events or cackle your approval of the latest joke or funny story making the rounds. Your best bet is to say to your friends that you should have a coffee after you've finished your auditions. You don't want to be the person who ruins someone else's audition, nor do you want to be the person whose audition is ruined by a rowdy crowd.

Another more insidious reason for avoiding discussion before your audition is the danger of jealous friends. Beware of a "friend" who quietly mentions that you look like you've put on weight. Ignore the "friend" who confides that his agent swore the casting director said he was the perfect person for the role you are both auditioning for. Don't listen to someone who says he heard you were cleaning houses. The motive for saying these things is purposely to try to psych you out. If you don't engage in discussion outside the audition room, you won't have to listen.

5: DO "TAKE 1" OUTSIDE THE DOOR.

One of the things I tell actors in my workshop is that you should always be ready to deliver "Take 2" once you get called in. You should be preparing yourself while you are waiting, and be so ready that when you get in front of the camera, you've already done the preliminary and rough first take just for yourself. You should be getting into character and trying to relax while you're waiting to be called. So once you step inside the room, you are ready to deliver your perfected "Take 2."

6: DON'T DISAPPEAR.

If you need to be by yourself, you can go into a stairwell or the washroom after you've checked in, but let them know where you're going so you can be found when they're ready for you. Regardless, be back in the waiting room five minutes before your appointed time. And while you're sitting there, don't angst over the varying amounts of time they spend after each auditioner. Don't compare them. Sometimes an audition can trigger a discussion about a line in the script or about location or possible wardrobe problems. Not every discussion is about the actor. Sometimes there is no discussion at all. So don't second-guess how much time you think they will take between performers. Be there and be ready.

7: DON'T WASTE EVERYONE'S TIME: LEAVE ALL YOUR BAGGAGE OUTSIDE THE DOOR.

Make sure that you take off your coat and anything else you want to remove before you come in. If we've scheduled one person every five minutes, we don't want to waste time watching you pull off your gloves one finger at a time, then unwind your scarf from around your neck, and then finally undo the buttons on your coat one by one. Leave it all outside the door. Leave it with your gym bag and the purchases made on the way to the audition. I can tell you that the more you bring into the room, the more likely you are to forget something. If there's anything more difficult than coming into the audition room the first time, it's having to knock on the door and come in a second time to retrieve the hat you inadvertently left behind.

8: DON'T WASTE EVERYONE'S TIME: COMPLETE ALL YOUR PREPARATIONS BEFORE YOU ARE CALLED IN.

Several years ago, I had an audition where the scene was supposed to take place at a restaurant. An actor came in with a gym bag. From it she took a bottle of ginger ale (which she poured into a champagne glass), a plate, a knife, a fork, a spoon, and a napkin. Then she put a piece of bread on the plate, cut it with the knife and fork, and ate it all during her audition. I thought the producers and the director were going to die of boredom watching her set out all her trappings. This has the same negative effect as renting a uniform for an audition. While it's nice to show you care, it makes us wonder if you intend to dazzle us with your preparation because you really don't know how to act the scene. It's all just a waste of time, and wasting time is counterproductive.

Once, when I was casting a film set in the 1950s, we were looking for a teenage boy and girl. The scene we were using had a lovely bit of dialogue that took place in the back seat of a car while the two of them were necking. As written, the girl removes her panties from under her skirt and hangs them on the steering wheel, to the shock and amazement of the boy. All the girls we saw mimed the action of pulling down their panties. We had read dozens of kids for these two parts when one young woman came in close to the end of the day. She was delightful in the scene, and when she got to the part where she was supposed to remove her panties she mimed the action of pulling them down just as everyone else had done, but then in a flash she revealed a tiny pair of bikini underwear that had been scrunched into her hand the whole time. It was very effective. I can assure you that when we were recapping at the end of the day, we all remembered her.

9: BRING YOUR PICTURE AND RÉSUMÉ TO EVERY SINGLE AUDITION YOU EVER GO TO.

Casting Myth #6: Your agent has already sent your picture and résumé ahead of time so you don't need to bring them with you to the audition. You should never show up at an audition without your picture and résumé. Don't leave home without them. In the old days, before so much of the casting process was done on-line, we received the agents' suggestions with hard copies of the pictures and résumés. It was up to me to pull all the photos and résumés of the actors I had called in so I could present them to the director at the audition. Directors always want to look at the credits. (Sometimes I think they're just checking to see if any of their previous shows are mentioned, but nevertheless, they want that résumé in front of them.) Even back then you were supposed to bring your picture and résumé every time, just in case your agent hadn't sent one, or in case we liked you so much we asked for a second copy. But I don't receive those hard copies now. It's up to the actor to provide them when he arrives.

When I call out auditions, I tell the agents to please remind their clients to bring a photo and résumé. When I send out the sides, I write on the front page, "Please bring photo and résumé to audition." I actually have a stamp with that message, so it is clearly visible on the front page. Yet there are still actors who come to auditions without their photo and résumé. Why would you do that? When we recap at the end of the day, it's the photo that the director refers to if he doesn't remember someone. Yes, we do have the tape and yes, he will watch the tape later, but for that instant he wants to look at the picture. I can tell you that people have sometimes been forgotten because they didn't bring a photo. So don't leave home without it. I know that photos are expensive, but they are one of the tools of the trade for an actor.[1] Don't be stingy with them.

When you get to the audition, have your picture and résumé ready. I have seen actors who've been sitting there for thirty or forty minutes and when I call them in for their turn they ask if I need a picture and résumé. Yes, I need the picture! And I need it stapled and ready. That's why I stamped the front of the sides. After I say yes, off they go to their briefcases, searching through to find the photo and correct résumé as if it were a surprise that I want it. Or they find that the résumé is not up to date so they search for a pen and start writing in the recent credits. This takes time and slows everything down while I'm trying to keep the pace going and get the actors into the room as soon as possible. Besides, if the night before they had prepared a response to being asked what they have been doing lately (see Chapter 3), they would have checked then and found that something was missing. It should have been written in at that time, not when it means keeping a room full of people waiting.

So do yourself a big favour and make everyone happy by having your picture and résumé up to date, stapled, and ready when you arrive at the audition.

10: TAKE A DEEP BREATH.

The door to the audition room opens and you hear your name. This is it. Remember to exhale, get up from your chair, and go knock 'em dead!

CHAPTER NOTES

1. When I no longer need the photos, I recycle them. There's actually a company called Saving Face which provides that service. I call them when I have several big bags of photos to be returned and they pick them up, sort them, and deliver them to the actors' agencies. It costs ten cents per item, but that's a lot less than the $1.50 or $2.00 it costs for the picture in the first place. It's well worth it.

show time

SHOW TIME

THE ETIQUETTE OF THE ROOM

You know how every party usually has someone who's really good at "working the room"? That's what you have to learn to do once you step inside the door—work the room. Your clue as to how to do this should be taken from the person who escorts you in. In most cases it's the casting director, but sometimes it's an assistant. Come quickly when your name is called and then follow your escort into the room. She will introduce you to the people assembled, sometimes just by your first name. First names are enough because everyone in the room has a list and they can see who's next. If your escort introduces everyone else—producers, director, writer—that's great. If she doesn't, don't bother to ask who they are. You only need to know who will be reading with you. If it isn't obvious, then ask. But usually it's obvious.

Every audition room has its own personality. Sometimes it's easy and relaxed; sometimes it's tense and pressured. If the room is silent, it's not a good idea to try to liven it up with a joke. If everyone is easygoing and chatty, you can be too. But take your cues from what you find.

You can also take your cues from the material you've been given to read. When Danny DeVito saw the character of the dispatcher in *Taxi*, he decided to use it:

Actors occasionally take unusual steps to break the ice with jaded casting agents [*sic*]. When Danny DeVito auditioned for *Taxi*, he marched into a tension-filled room packed with network executives, slammed the script down on a table, and shouted, "Before I start, I have a question to ask: *Who wrote this shit?*" He didn't have to read a line after that.[1]

What DeVito did was to come into the room already in character. That's great as long as you let the director know that it is a character that you've assumed. You don't want him to think that you really are a bitch if you've taken on the character of a bitch. He might not want to work with you if he thinks you're going to be too difficult. So when your audition is finished, you might try reverting to your natural sweet self and ask, "Was that what you were looking for?"

The same is true of dialects and accents. If you want to wow them with your brilliant accent by using it before you start the scene, let them know that you can lose the accent in case they don't like it and want to hear you do it again in your own voice. Even American accents should be treated in this way.

Oh, the things I've heard actors say when they first sit down. It's astounding. It's not a good idea to start an audition by saying, "I'm really not right for this, but here goes nothing!" as one actor said to me. Many will gush about the script and how much they love it. Sometimes someone will go on about how much they hate it. I've been in a room where one actor lectured all of us about something he found objectionable in the script. I've heard actors go on about how much this role means to them because something just like this happened to their mother or cousin or friend. I've even heard actors plead for the part because they haven't been working much lately and they need the money. Oh boy!

While I understand the temptation to compliment a script you really love, *be careful*. If the script is good, then it would be fine to say simply, "I loved the script." But if the script is lousy, almost everyone will know you're lying. That's not good. Nor is it good to make disparaging comments about a bad script because the writer may be in the room and he may think it's wonderful even if no one else does. Let's face it, we've all had to work on projects that we want to disavow later, but we all have to eat. So if everyone in the room knows that a script is pretty bad, but each person took the gig for his own private reasons, the last thing anyone wants is to be reminded that this project will probably not be prominent on the résumé.

It may happen that once or twice in your acting career, you get called in to audition for something you find just too objectionable. Perhaps it's racist or sexist or too violent for your taste. It might even be too risqué and not something you would be comfortable with. If that's the case you should not go to the audition. The union agreement states that if nudity is required for a role, that requirement must be communicated before the audition so there won't be any surprises. Don't go to the audition pretending you don't know about it. And don't go there with the intention of lecturing the filmmakers or thinking you will be able to change their minds. You can tell your agent the truth and the agent will decide what to say to the casting director. But you must tell your agent.

You can't just *not* show up. And you can't decide not to go on the morning of the audition when you have had the sides for two or three days. If you're going to cancel, make sure you get in touch the day before, at the very latest.

I have no trouble at all being told that someone can't relate to the material for whatever reason and doesn't want to come in. But if you accept the invitation, then you have to be prepared to come to the party. If you come to the party, then be prepared to act. If you do a good job, then you'll be remembered for it. If you come in with attitude, then you have just introduced yourself to four or five or six people who will probably never call you in again.

THE EXECUTION

The only things you should have with you when you walk into the room are your purse or wallet and the things you need for your audition. So if you've decided to use a prop or aid of some kind, it's with you when you walk in. But don't forget the most important aid of all—your sides. In Chapter 3, I urged you always to memorize your sides. And so you should. But auditions are a lot more stressful than actually playing the scene once you have the part. If you're nervous, you're liable to dry up and forget every word you knew so well in the waiting room or in front of your mirror at home. I have seen actors auditioning for two lines who have become so frozen with nerves that they couldn't even remember what the scene was about. You must have your pages with you. You don't have to keep them in your hand; you can spread them out on the floor in front of you, or if you intend to stand you can put them on the seat of the chair so you can sneak a glance once in a while. Sometimes people like having them in their hands just to steady the nervous shakes.

You can't always count on the reader to help you out if you forget your lines or get confused. Sometimes the reader is an actor hired for the day, or the casting director who has a vested interest in making you look good and can help you out (see Chapter 2). But sometimes the reader is just a production assistant corralled into doing this because there was no one else available. If that's the case, he won't know if you have just taken a dramatic pause or really need help. Don't rely on him. If you have to stop and ask to look at a copy of the sides, or go searching in your pockets to find your crumpled pages, the moment will be lost. Have your sides in view—just in case.

The first thing you should do is go to the chair offered to you and sit down. Even if you intend to stand for the audition, you should be ready to chat first. Maybe, as discussed earlier, it's to answer the question, "What have you been doing lately?" Or maybe the director will ask if you have any questions.

That is a minefield.

Imagine: You got your sides yesterday and spent all last night doing the preparation. You made up anything you didn't have answers for so your character could be complete. You were absolutely ready with all your choices made. But then you get to the audition and the director asks if you have any questions. You take a chance and ask what happened in the scene just previous to this one. He tells you and you discover that it throws your preparation out the window. Every question you answered for yourself was based on what you made up and now you find that what you made up is exactly the opposite of the reality. If you asked, you have to be prepared to use what you are told.

So don't ask. Hold off on questions that relate to motivation or back story.

The one question you should always ask is about pronunciation. In Chapter 3, I said that your preparation should include looking up anything in the dictionary that you don't understand. But if there's a word you don't know how to pronounce, a place name or a person's name, you should ask how to say it before you begin the scene. Once you're given the correct pronunciation, repeat it out loud several times, just to fix it firmly in your head and on your lips. If you don't ask, when you get to that word you'll stumble and maybe even have to stop. It will spoil your concentration and take you and the listeners right out of the scene.

So ask about pronunciation, but leave any questions of motivation or back story until after you show them your first take. If you don't get a second one, you will have shown all your preparation and given your best shot.

Be prepared for anything at this point. The director may see something on your résumé that prompts a question. He may ask what your favourite acting job has been. Maybe he will ask what it was like to work with a certain director or actor. Or maybe you were in some exotic location he wants to know about. But it's the simple questions that will likely trip you up if you aren't careful.

I remember one audition where the actor was reading for a part in a series that had already been on the air for a couple of years. The director asked if the actor was familiar with the show and the actor replied, "Oh, I don't watch television." That's just the wrong answer. Besides the fact that it's stupid, it shows that you didn't do one part of the preparation: you didn't make yourself familiar with the show. Part of an actor's homework is knowing what is going on around him. Certainly knowing all the locally made television shows currently on the air is useful and important. If the scene you are reading is with the lead of the series, how much easier it will be for you to audition if you know the actor who would be playing opposite you.

This is your audition. You should make yourself as comfortable as possible under the circumstances. That means the choice is yours whether to stand or sit. Or you may decide to do both. If you do or if you're going to walk around within the scene, let the camera operator know. Sometimes he locks off the camera and if he doesn't know that you intend to move around, there will be a few frames where the screen is empty while the operator searches for your face. Check out where the best lighting is and don't move beyond it. Usually the chair has been strategically placed to give you the best lighting, so ask how far you can move.

The same is true for the sound. Good audition facilities will have a microphone placed so that both voices will be heard clearly. If it's suspended, make sure you won't bang into it. If it's placed on a stand near you, you don't want to put anything over it. I have often seen actors place their sides on the stand that holds the mic. Resist the temptation. Put the sides elsewhere.

Finally! All that preparation leads to this. You're ready to begin. First the slate. Many casting facilities today will put the slate on screen electronically with a character generator. If that's the case then they will tell you that you don't have to slate and you can just start the scene in your own time. If you do have to slate, look directly into the camera and state your name and your agent. That's all you need and that's the last time you will look directly into the lens. Take a beat and direct your attention to the reader. Start whenever you are ready. And don't forget to breathe. You don't have to rush to begin. This is your moment. Take it.

The hurdle you have to jump now is the stage directions. The best thing you can do for yourself is to ignore them. Keep it simple.

I had an audition scene a while ago where a woman was supposed to answer a knock at her kitchen door carrying a crying baby and the baby's bottle. That's what was written on the page. I watched as one actor after another mimed opening the imaginary screen door of the kitchen, holding it open with her foot, cradling the imaginary baby in one arm and clutching the imaginary bottle with the other hand. It was quite a long scene and as it progressed, I watched as each actor forgot about the door or dropped the baby. Not a pretty sight.

This is not an exercise in pantomime. If you do decide to "carry a baby," you have to remember not to drop it halfway through the scene. It's much easier to ignore the stage directions at this point. If you want, you can announce before you start that you intend to ignore them unless directed otherwise. Remember that the audition process is to see what you look like, hear what you sound like, and to get an idea of how you would approach the material. If you get the part, you'll be provided with a real baby on the day. (Please don't drop it!)

You also want to ignore any stage directions that tell you to smoke. You can certainly bring an unlit cigarette into the room, but obviously, lighting up in most places today can get you thrown in jail. I know it seems preposterous, but not so long ago I saw actors light a cigarette and then when it wasn't needed any more, they'd stamp it out on the floor or the carpet. Not a good idea. But something much more innocuous can also cause a lot of grief. Be careful of chewing gum. If you have to remove it, there is often no place to put it and you have to hold on to it until you leave the room. Or you risk forgetting about it and chewing it all through another scene where it is entirely misplaced. Even drinking water during a scene can be problematic. If it goes down the wrong way you'll have to stop because you're choking.

When we watch auditions, we need to see your eyes. The reader is positioned precisely so that the eye line is perfect and gives a full view of your face. If it happens that you have not had a chance to memorize the sides completely, you still have to find opportunities to look at the reader. You should also be conscious of eye line if you have worked out any business that moves you too far from your mark. Sometimes eye line is tricky if you're reading a scene where you are supposed to be talking to two people but there is only one reader. My advice is to pretend you're only talking to one person. It's too confusing to talk to one person and then look at a point on the wall for the second person when the voice is only coming from one place. Just use the reader. Keep it simple.

It never occurred to me when I became a casting director that I would need danger pay. But on occasion, while reading with actors, I have been kissed, stroked, caressed, strangled, hit, thrown against the wall, and even tackled. It's not a good idea to touch the reader. Really. Resist the temptation. No matter what the stage directions say, don't touch the reader. The reader is supposed to be helping you, but how can I help you if I can't breathe? Once, when I got kissed during an audition, I became so flustered that I completely lost my place and couldn't get back into the scene. If you get the part, you'll be able to smooch with a real actor on the day. So no matter what the stage directions say, don't touch the reader.

If there are five or six people behind the table, it's safe to say that one of them is probably the writer. Writers really don't like it when you change their dialogue, particularly if the scene is a comedy. I have heard actors improve on a joke in an audition or, on occasion, even add a bit of humour. These additions are often really funny, but the writer will be furious. Egos sometimes are pretty fragile. While everyone understands that you may want to change the odd thing, you should try as much as possible to stick to the text.

When I'm reading with an actor and the scene is finished, I usually announce the end by looking up and saying "Scene." I don't like to say "Cut," because that's the prerogative of the director. One of the best things you can teach yourself to do is to hold on to your last pose for several beats after the end of the scene. This is something that will serve you well not only in auditions but also in any role you get. First of all, in auditions the natural tendency is to grimace and make a funny face at the end of a take to show that you think you didn't do a very good job, or perhaps to signal that you feel you can do better. What you are looking for is a chance at a second take. But what happens is that the camera operator will turn off the camera when he hears me say "Scene." If you are sticking out your tongue, that is the last image of you that will be captured on tape. I don't really think that's the impression you wish to leave. It's not a good idea to grimace at your own performance in any case, but especially not before you are sure that the camera has been turned off.

I have often heard producers and directors say that an actor has really helped them out in the editing room by holding on to his final pose at the end of a take. When they are editing, they are sometimes looking for any extra frame of usable material they can find. They may need the picture to hold on you for two seconds because of a sound effect or a music cue or another person's line of dialogue. If you've jumped out too soon, they will scramble to find another solution. You want every nanosecond of screen time you can get, so this is a good habit to learn right at the audition. Hold your final pose longer than might seem natural at the time.

DIRECTORS

Casting Myth #7: Directors always know how to communicate to the actors exactly what they are looking for. Is that ever wishful thinking! My job would be so much easier if directors always knew what they were looking for. In fact, so would yours. The truth is that very often they haven't got a clue. And if they do, they don't know how to share it with you.

One of the wonderful benefits of being a casting director is that I get to work with different people all the time. As a result, I have compiled my own personal list of the types of directors who are out there. It is by no means definitive. You can add to it if you'd like.

#1: THE FIRST TIMER

He's usually young, but not always. He's nervous and, although you might not believe this, maybe even more nervous than you. Even experienced directors tend to get nervous at the beginning of a new project. So he's jittery and fumbling and not expressing himself well. That might make you feel a little better or it might have the opposite effect and make you even less confident. But whatever the effect, he will not be much help to you.

#2: THE BOOR

This guy is very busy eating pistachios while you're doing your scene. Or maybe he is reading the *National Enquirer* and making a big noise turning the pages. He's also the guy who forgets to turn off his cellphone before you start. Then he doesn't even bother to look up at you when you leave the room. It isn't because your audition was bad—I promise you. It's because the guy is a jerk. Ignore him. Just do your thing and get out of there.

#3: THE BORE

Different from the Boor, this guy might be very well intentioned. He just talks too much and doesn't say anything. Or he says way more than you can absorb. He might get very caught up in telling you the back story for your character or he might even want to give you the synopsis of the whole plot. Then when it comes time actually to direct what you are doing, he doesn't have anything to say. Not much help to be had here.

#4: MR. L.A.

He's usually wearing sunglasses and doesn't ever remove them. Often his feet are resting up on the table. He'll suddenly remember, between takes, that he has to make an urgent phone call to "The Coast," whip out his tiny cellphone, and loudly discuss his next gig with his agent. He uses terms like "pithy" and "sense memory" and doesn't give you any direction you can use. So again, you are on your own.

#5: INSCRUTABLE

This guy will show nothing at all. You won't know if he liked what you did, if he hated what you did, or if he even saw what you did. You come into the room, he doesn't ask questions, you start your audition, he says "Thanks," and you're dismissed. No notes, no discussion, and no "Take 2." You feel shell-shocked as you slink towards the door.

#6: THE "TECHNICAL" DIRECTOR

There are those directors who have made their reputations on their facility with the technical aspects of film-making. They may be excellent at working with special effects and all the new technologies. That's great, and they may turn out exciting adventure movies. They just don't know how to work with actors and that becomes evident at the audition. They have a vision in their heads and they know how they will execute the scene. They just aren't able to share it with you.

#7: THE ACTORS' DIRECTOR

He's the opposite of #6. He knows exactly what to say to actors, maybe he came from the theatre. He just hasn't got a clue how he's going to shoot this sucker.

#8: THE EAGER BEAVER

He's just so excited to be here and doing this wonderful work. He's thrilled to meet you and hear all about the great things on your résumé. He asks about every director you have ever worked with and all the exotic locations you have visited. All you want is for him to shut up so you can get on with your audition. When he does finally stop talking, he still hasn't given you any direction to speak of.

#9: MR. BEEN THERE DONE THAT

This guy may be very nice and courteous, he just appears tired. He's been doing it for so long that nothing surprises him and nothing really moves him any more. You do your audition and if it's a comic scene and everyone else in the room is laughing, or even just smiling, he shows absolutely nothing. It's as if he just wishes he could go home and take a nap.

#10: THE OVERSTATER

This guy could also be called "He who makes promises he can't keep." We all know someone like this. He's effusive and tells you that you are perfect for the part. He says your audition was outstanding. He practically gives you the part on the spot. Only you don't ever hear from him and the part goes to someone else. Be wary of anyone who offers too much praise at an audition.

#11: NO DIRECTOR PRESENT

Personally, I like this one. When there is no director (or producer) at the audition, then it's the casting director who runs the show. You almost always find that a casting director will spend more time and give more direction than a director. That's because the director is focused only on the role in question for the present project. The casting director usually has a larger view. I want to put every actor into the memory bank, so if it doesn't work out for this show I will know how to cast this actor somewhere else.

#12: THE GOOD DIRECTOR

He asks you a question or two to put you at your ease. He lets you do your audition without discussion so he can see your preparation. He says something positive so you feel confident, and then he gives you a single, simple note letting you know what he wants for "Take 2." He actually knows what he wants and can express himself. He might work on the scene a bit more. But even if he doesn't, you will leave feeling that you had a good audition, that he was attentive and courteous. He'll say "Thank you" when you leave and perhaps even "Goodbye." These guys are rare, but they do exist.

I often get invited to do audition seminars with new directors and new producers. I love meeting the future movers and shakers and telling them how it should be done, how much more they can achieve if they show a little courtesy and are prepared and can articulate what they want from the actors in auditions. I wish I could tell all directors.

With the exception of #11 and #12, the one common trait of the others is that you can't count on them for much. You're on your own out there and if you've taken shortcuts with your preparation, you'll be hung out to dry. The bottom line is to be so well prepared that you don't need the director at all for the audition. You've done what you have to do and it will show whether he helps you or not. But if you are lucky enough to have an audition with Director #12, you better take full advantage of the situation.

When people are really nervous, their ability to listen is often impaired. If you are confronted with a good director or, even more importantly, a director who talks too much, you have to make yourself concentrate really hard to hear what he is saying to you. I've heard actors tell me that when the director spoke, it was like looking at one of those old movies where the lips are moving but the sound has become fuzzy and you can't make out what is being said. So just try to locate the one important detail in all the verbiage that's coming at you. This is the most important test in the audition. *If the director gives you direction, you must take it.* If he asks you to make an adjustment, you better make the change. The worst thing you can do at that moment is to do it again the same way. He's looking to see how well you take direction, no matter how well he gives it, and if you don't take it at all, you won't get the part.

There is, however, one exception. There are times when the director will ask you to do it again exactly the same way. Maybe he liked what you did and wants to see if you can give it a bit more energy by rolling right into a second take immediately. Or maybe he wants to see if you can be consistent take after take in case there is a problem on set that necessitates a lot of takes. If you start changing what you're doing from take to take when you're meant to keep it the same, you will not be popular with anyone. The continuity person, the lighting crew, the sound people will all be counting on you. You can't let them down. The director might just be testing that skill at the audition.

I know it seems like there are a lot of traps you can fall into. That's because there are.

CHUTZPAH

Chutzpah means nerve. How much do you have? When you are dismissed from one of those ghastly auditions where no one has said anything or given you a chance to do it again, you can take control of the situation, if you have the courage. You have every right to ask gently, "May I try it again?" Or, "Is there something else you would like to see?" You really don't risk very much. After all, they can only say no. I have heard directors answer, "Thanks, but I think we've got what we need." However sometimes they will be so surprised that they will answer, "Sure."

Here again, you have to be smart. If you ask to do another take, you better improve on what you did before. Your best bet is to ask if they would like something different or should you just do it the same way. Then listen carefully to the answer and do what they tell you. If the scene is very long, they might stop you halfway through. Don't worry. It's probably just a question of time.

There's another gutsy thing you can try if the role you are reading for is small. Let's say your one line is, "Matt, there's a call for you in the front office." You announce to the room that you have prepared it a few different ways and then, without pausing, just reel them off. "Here it is very professional and straightforward." "Here it is perky." "Here it is nervous." "Here it is angry." You have to be fairly bold to carry that one off, but you have nothing to lose. You haven't wasted their time, and if you really show what you set out to show each time, then you will have accomplished something.

When you are preparing the sides, you may find that one obvious choice presents itself. If you can see an alternative to the obvious and you can execute it well, it's worth preparing that too. Then when you get into the room, you can, if you're confident enough, say that you have prepared it the obvious way, but you would also like to try something a little different. Then the choice is theirs. Maybe they really want the obvious and don't have time to play around. But maybe they are willing to have a look at something else. If it doesn't work, they will ask you to do it the way everyone else is doing it. For that reason I always think you should be ready to do it both ways if you are choosing something you know is way out there. And don't just be prepared, let them know you're prepared. Then don't worry if the unusual choice doesn't work. If you do the "straight-up" choice well, you will still be remembered for having tried something different.

There is one move that really requires *cojones*. I have auditioned actors who come into the room already in character. They maintain that character through the chat, the audition, the retakes, and the departure. If that character has a lisp or a speech impediment, or if he limps or has a tick, you risk that the people in the room won't know if that's really you or the character. They might fear that if the tic doesn't work for the role, you won't be able to lose it. If you don't know anyone in the room who can vouch for the fact that you are *acting,* I think it's better to come in as yourself and then assume your character. Or you can come in in character and when you have finished your audition you can say, "Is that what you were looking for, or would you like to see it without the tics?" However, if you do know someone in the room, it's a bold move that can be extremely effective. You can also use the same approach with accents.

If you don't feel you can pull off any of these bold moves, don't worry about it. Just do what you are asked to do, do it well, and you'll be fine.

And here's something to hold in your memory bank for the future. There is one sure thing you can always do to improve an audition: *speed it up.* I understand why most auditions are too slow. It's because you've had twenty-four hours to angst over it. You've studied and memorized and created a character and now you finally get a chance to show what you've prepared and what you can do. The temptation to drag it out for as long as possible is enormous. But don't. Act with the lines, not in the pauses between them. Don't let a ponderous, slow reading be your downfall.

THE DEPARTURE

When you've done all you can and it's time to leave the room, just say "Thank you" and leave. Make sure you take all your belongings out with you so you don't have to come in again. It's not the time to gush about what a wonderful opportunity this has been. It's not the time to get into a discussion about your availability. It's not the time to tell the assembled crowd why you think you deserve the role. Keep your dignity. It's also not necessary to shake everyone's hand before departing. If you've scattered your pages around the floor, pick them up before leaving, and get out as quickly as possible.

They may not even acknowledge your departure. At that point they are busy writing their notes about your performance. All they want to do is keep the session going.

They are looking towards the end of the day when they can get out of there. So if no one looks up or says anything, it doesn't mean it's a sign of how badly you did. In fact, it can mean that they are busy noting how much they liked your audition. In any case, there's nothing further you can do so just leave and try to forget all about it.

CHAPTER NOTES

1. Trish Deitch Rohrer, *Premiere Magazine*, February 1990

MARSHA CHESLEY

when the lights are turned off, what goes on?

WHEN THE LIGHTS ARE TURNED OFF, WHAT GOES ON?

C asting Myth #8: All casting decisions are obvious and clear and can be made easily. "David Rubin, an independent casting director, says, 'I wish the casting process was filled with more of those revelatory moments, when somebody comes in and is so immediately the answer. It's not. It usually comes down to lots of deliberation and an occasional compromise. It's not about those golden moments.' "[1]

Once in a long while the right person just walks in the door and everyone feels it. Something magical happens. Most of the time there is lots of discussion, there are major compromises, and usually an inordinate amount of arbitrariness. It's hard to make decisions when so much is riding on them. We've all seen films completely ruined by bad casting. Nothing can save them. Perhaps the most glaring error in recent years was when Brian de Palma cast Tom Hanks in *Bonfire of the Vanities*. It had been a much-loved book written by Tom Wolfe, but the hero was nothing like Tom Hanks. "Master of the Universe" Sherman McCoy (even the name doesn't suit Hanks) was meant to be sharp-edged and greedy, whereas Hanks is so wholesome and likeable. The disconnect was just too great. The movie was a colossal failure in spite of Hanks and de Palma and an all-star supporting cast. No matter how good an actor is, if he is wrong for the part it just won't work.

After a casting session has ended, the decision process starts in earnest.

Casting Myth #9: The casting director makes all decisions about who should be cast in every role. This is a common misconception. Final decisions never rest with the casting director. And that's the way it should be. After all, it's the producer's money and it's the director who is on the floor with the actors on the day. But wise producers and directors will consult with the casting director, and decisions will be collaborative. How much influence the casting director has depends on her relationship with the producer and the director. If they've all worked together several times, there will be a level of trust and confidence. Good producers and directors know that they get to go through the casting process maybe once a year, if they're lucky enough to get a project financed once a year. A casting director is involved in casting every single day. Even if I'm not working on a specific project I'm still familiarizing myself with talent, both new and old, on a constant basis.

I'm also able to offer advice about the kind of performance an actor gave at his audition. Since I have seen most of the established actors dozens of times, I'm able to comment on whether the audition given was up to his usual standard or not. I can offer a word or two about an actor's versatility or range. These are things it's my job to know that will help in the decision-making process.

So we begin by going through the list of auditioners in order of appearance, and we look at the photos just to jog the memory. If a photo is missing, (i.e., the actor forgot it on his kitchen table), the actor sometimes goes missing as well. That actor must be very good and really well known to the director in order to remain in the running if the photo is missing. If the audition was just adequate, the director won't bother to go back and look at the tape.

The easiest way for us to begin is by eliminating the obvious rejects for each role. Then the remaining two or three are discussed. Here are some comments I've heard regarding individual actors:

"I really liked him."

"I didn't like him."

"Wasn't he too old for the part?"

"Wasn't he too thin for the part?"

"I thought he did a really nice audition."

"I thought he was awful."

"He wasn't right for the part."

"Who does he have to play opposite?"

"Who can we pair him up with?"

"There's nobody."

"Maybe there's somebody."

"Can we see some more people?"

Hmm. Not much to go on there.

At this point, it makes a difference whether the casting session has been for a feature or movie-of-the-week, or episodic television. When we have the luxury of time, we will use this session to start eliminating people, but not necessarily making final selections. We usually agree to hold on to the two or three we like and continue to see more people. After we have seen enough to satisfy everyone, we will narrow down the list and decide if we want callbacks or tape on these people. Of course it does happen that we cast someone on the spot, or once we have the short list a decision will be made without callbacks. In looking at all the possibilities, if one actor seems the right choice, then we go with it.

Time is very short in episodics. I usually get one four-hour session with the director to cast a one-hour episode. That can be anywhere from twelve to twenty roles, or in the case of one series I worked on there were approximately thirty-five roles per episode. If more time is needed, then I often conduct the session myself and send the tape to the producer and the director. But most of the decisions have to be made at that one session. So I have to get everyone to focus and decide.

Usually one part is the lead, or guest star, and even in an ensemble piece there is one part that is the anchor. We have to start there and then fit all the pieces around that one. Once that first decision is made, many of the other choices often depend on things that are not necessarily based on how good or bad an audition was. If we have to match family members we try to cast actors with some kind of resemblance to each other. So if the family is blond and you are a redhead or brunette, you won't be cast. There are occasions where the age of the anchor colours the age of a whole group if all the members of the group need to be the same age. If the best auditioners for other parts were considerably older than the lead, those others might not get the parts. Of course with couples, chemistry has to play a part. Some pairs have it and some just don't. As in real life, there is no explaining chemistry.

There are so many permutations and combinations of reasons for decisions that it's impossible to relate them all. I know it's hard to believe, but it's true that in most cases the reason an actor does not get the part is *not* because he did a bad audition.

There are situations where people from other walks of life are turned into actors. Perhaps the lead female is a prima ballerina and instead of using doubles we want to cast a dancer. In that case, actors would be auditioned as well—just in case we don't find a dancer capable of the acting requirements. If a dancer gets the role, then obviously the actors who auditioned will not. I've also cast a film where the lead role was a high-fashion model. In my opinion, it's always best to cast an actor, but in this case they decided to go with a model and try to teach her to act. Actors were auditioned, as well, and in all honesty they were almost all better than the model who did get the part.

There are also those unfortunate situations where the casting of a role is complete and the director has made his decision. Then a network or distributor or executive producer steps in and dictates that the lead should be a bigger "name." Obviously the "no-name" actor will not get hired even though he auditioned brilliantly.

A famous Canadian director told me about a situation he experienced when he was just starting out. The producers had their one "name" actor in the lead and the director needed to cast a daughter for her. They auditioned lots of actors and found one they were all thrilled with. Then the network stepped in and decided that the one "name" they had was not enough. They gave the director another actor they said had a big enough "name," to play the part of the daughter. No one had ever heard of her. So much for a "name." But during the course of the shoot, the director found that she was an excellent actress and they became friends. In the middle of the shoot, she told him that she had to go to Los Angeles for the weekend because she was testing for a really big part. He was happy for her and wished her luck. On Monday he was eager to find out what had happened with her audition. She told him that she had gone down to L.A. but she had not had the chance to audition at all because the producers of the project had decided they needed a "name" actress for the role. Hmm...

Perhaps the most difficult thing for an actor to hear is just how arbitrary a process casting can be. Film-making is collaborative, so people have to compromise in order to get things done. In an effort to compromise, deals are often made. They don't really think of them as deals, but that's what they are. You will often hear a producer say, "Okay, I gave you your choice for the part of Bob, so now you give me mine for the part of Sal." Or, "I gave you the gaffer, now you give me an actor." And the deal is done. Unfortunately, there is a possibility that the person who gave the best audition for Bob or Sal did not get the part.

A real frustration for me is auditioning a big, juicy role for a woman over forty years old. Those parts are so rare that when I get the opportunity, I bring in as many as possible of the wonderfully talented women who so seldom get a chance to strut their stuff. The end result is that they are all fantastic and any one of them could and should do the role. But we can only choose one. So all the other deserving women will have to wait for another day. If I'm frustrated by that, imagine how they feel.

So you know that auditions are brutal. They are also cruel. And they can be unfair as well. I've filled this book with all the reasons you have to perform better than everybody else if you want to win the role. I've told you that you have to be bold, different, uninhibited, and memorable. And now I'm telling you that even if you do all those things to perfection, you still may not get the part. You can give your best and very often it doesn't seem to matter.

All this just adds to the bitter pill of rejection on which the whole business is based. It's worth repeating that if you can't take a good dose of rejection, you probably want to consider a different career path. Perhaps the consolation is that if you have done the best you can, you will be remembered. That's why, every single time you are given the opportunity to audition you have to seize it firmly and make the absolute most of it. Make every audition an opportunity for more people to see you perform and hopefully remember you later on for something else.

Casting Myth #10: "We both auditioned for the part. He got it, I didn't. Obviously he can act and I stink. I should quit now and give up this business altogether."

Everything I've said in the last few pages is to illustrate that the above statement really is just a myth. I hope that by learning about all the deals that are made and all the reasons that some people are cast and some aren't, that bitter pill will be a little easier to swallow and your paranoia and frustration will be lessened. I hope it's something of a consolation to know that just because you didn't get the part, it doesn't mean your audition was bad. It doesn't mean that you stink and should give up the business. But regardless of all the deals and compromises, your job is still to make your audition stand out from the crowd in some way. You will never lose by doing that. You will sometimes win the role. But even if you don't, you will have won something else—a room full of admirers who will think well of you in the future.

CHAPTER NOTES

1. Trish Deitch Rohrer, *Premiere Magazine*, February 1990

demo reels, self-made tapes, and callbacks

DEMO REELS, SELF-MADE TAPES, AND CALLBACKS

DEMO REELS

So you had your audition yesterday and you think it went really well. Now you're in that place where you know you should just put this one behind you, not think too much about it, and focus on the next one. But you can't. You really think this was the one—the one where you put it all together, and you want to know what you can do next.

In Chapter 2, I mentioned demo reels as a tool to help get you an agent or perhaps to make your work available to casting directors who don't know you. But demo reels are also a very valuable tool when you've already auditioned and the producer or the director wants to see something else you've done.

Whenever you get a role on television or in a film, you should try to get access to a copy of the finished show as soon as it airs. Don't wait too long or you may not be able to find the people involved and you won't know how to track them down. You can always tape a show off the air and use that, but you lose a generation when you transfer it and the quality suffers. And quality does matter. So borrow the best quality tape they will lend you and make a professional transfer of your scenes.

The majority of demo reels given to me for consideration are not very good. Most actors feel the need to show an entire scene—beginning, middle, and end. That's counterproductive. Very often when you show the beginning, middle, and end of the scene, you only show more of the other actors. You have to be judicious and that usually means being brutal. Cut the scene to the bare bones to make sure that what is left shows *you*. I don't need to make sense of what's happening. I just have to see you at your best showing what you can do. If it's really short, that's great. A collection of thirty-second bits is all you want. I can tell you that if a scene goes on too long, the only thing that gets my full attention is my thumb—on the fast-forward button.

You should also be careful of including scenes where the other actor is someone who is your direct competition. There's no need to give suggestions to a producer whom you want to hire you.

If you consider the objective of the demo reel, it will make your task easier to accomplish. You want to show your range; you want to show both comedy and drama if you have it; you want to show all the wonderful co-stars you've appeared with. You want to show how good you are. So if you have six scenes where you play the young executive, and you're doing the same thing in each, choose the best one. Choose more if there are international stars in your scenes. It's to your credit if you get to work with great people and you should show it off.

Obviously the reel will change as you accumulate more credits, but at the beginning you have to go with what you've got. Keep it short and focused on you. When you do have several pieces to choose from, try not to be repetitive. If all you have is two good scenes that only add up to one and a half minutes, it's still worthwhile.

A personal word on montage sequences—most demo reels start with them and sometimes end with them as well. They are unnecessary. I usually fast forward until I get to the first real scene. Montages are very costly to include and I find them totally irrelevant. As far as I'm concerned they are a waste of time and money. Others like them, so make your own decision.

If you have a satisfactory demo reel, this is the point in the process to use it. If you had your audition yesterday and feel it went very well, you can get your agent to phone and offer your demo reel, which will show you doing other material and provide the director with a variety of scenes. You can make the case that the demo reel will show not only your versatility but that even under the pressure of working with a big star you were strong and effective. Sometimes I ask for a demo reel at this point, but if I don't, then get your agent to suggest that I look at yours.

A demo reel can also be used as a stand-in for an initial audition. If you are called in to audition but you happen to be out of town or working on another job, your agent can send in the demo reel instead. The only proviso is that the casting director must have the demo reel before the actual auditions take place or the part may already be cast.

Demo reels will rarely get an actor the job. They are just an extra little nudge to the decision-makers, in your favour. But don't worry if you don't have a demo reel. If you haven't done enough professional roles to make a decent reel, just wait until you do. Don't use scenes that don't show you well just for the sake of putting something on tape. Keep on doing your best at auditions and eventually you will have enough good credits to make a good reel.

One last comment on demo reels: Under no circumstance should you make your own demo reel and create scenes using your friends. Nor should you tape a monologue you have prepared for theatre auditions. These are not professional and shouldn't be shown.

SELF-MADE TAPES

This is a fairly new phenomenon but now a very common one. When people live in a city different from the one where the auditions are taking place, we often ask them to put themselves on tape using the sides we provide. This is different from a demo reel. We want to see you performing with our material. We fax or e-mail the sides, giving some useful direction. The ease of videotaping makes it possible and timely. Just to be clear, self-made tapes are tapes requested by a casting director for a specific project with sides from that particular script.

There are some things you should think about if you are going to put yourself on tape for a director in another city. As with demo reels, quality does count. So if you're going to use a home camera, make sure it's on a tripod and not hand-held. A shaky camera won't do for an audition. I've seen some that look like the camera operator had a very bad palsy. Also, make sure the background is plain. Remove pictures from the wall behind you and definitely remove any mirrors. Avoid harsh or strong directional lights because they will make any shadows under the eyes more pronounced. Test the sound quality. With most home cameras, the microphone is on the camera. What usually happens is that the reader who is standing beside the camera is heard perfectly while the auditioning actor who is farther away is fuzzy and barely audible. If that's the case, then you will have to stand closer to the camera—perhaps unnaturally close, but it can't be helped. Or the reader can stand behind the camera and slightly off to the side to make sure the eye line is okay. That will allow the auditioner to get closer to the microphone.

Framing is important as well. The shot should start out fairly wide—full body—and then move in. The majority of the scene should be in close-up. We want to see your face so we can evaluate your emotions from your expressions. We want to watch how well you listen. So if the shot remains too wide, we are frustrated and you aren't being seen to your best advantage.

One of the worst problems with self-made audition tapes is the reader. Don't have your roommate help you out if your roommate isn't an actor or has a learning disability that makes reading out loud a trial. Usually actors have some friends who are also actors, so try to use one of them. After all, if he helps you this time, you'll help him when his turn comes. A bad reader can make an audition unwatchable.

As with demo reels, timing can be crucial. I always ask for self-tapes to arrive before the actual auditions take place. When I have all the decision-makers in the room for the auditions, I will show them the tape. That way I can be sure they have watched it, but it also means that you have the same chance at being considered as the people who were actually in the room. If your tape arrives a day later, the part may already be cast and all the work you've done, not to mention the expense, will be for nothing.

When director Peter Jackson was being interviewed by Charlie Rose on PBS at the time he was doing the press for The *Lord of the Rings: The Fellowship of the Ring,* he said that he had had a very difficult time casting the role of Frodo Baggins. He had seen hundreds of actors on several continents without finding just what he was looking for. Elijah Wood heard about this and was convinced he was the right actor for the part and was determined to prove it to Jackson. Jackson was unfamiliar with Elijah Wood. He had not seen him in *The Ice Storm,* or any of the two dozen or so other films he had done to very high acclaim. So Wood got some help with wardrobe and makeup, then he climbed a tree and got a friend to videotape him as he recited lines from the book. He sent it to Jackson, and Jackson says he knew right away that his search was over. The way he put it—"Elijah Wood cast himself in *The Lord of the Rings.*" That was a self-tape with a twist. It could have failed but because it was done well, and because Wood was right for the role, it worked.

CALLBACKS

Callbacks are extremely important in the casting process. But in spite of that, I do believe that they are abused. When a director wants to call an actor back, it should be to see something more than he saw the first time. If he's only interested in having the actor do the same thing all over again, he should just review the tape of the first audition. Directors often forget that.

When you do get a callback, assume that you are being asked to show something different or to go more deeply into the role. If there's an extremely emotional scene in the film, I don't like to use it at the first audition. I find that it's much better to narrow the field and bring back just the contenders to dig down to the depths of their souls. If there's a scene where an actor has to have a nervous breakdown in front of us, it's painful for the actor but,

I can assure you, it's also painful for our side of the table: we have to watch it being done over and over again.

Make it your business to get a copy of the whole script when you get a callback. You should do all the same work you have to do for any audition, but this time dig deeper. There's more riding on it and you will have much less competition. Also, you have validation that someone thinks you are close to right for this part. Now you have to convince everybody that you are totally right for it.

Make sure you know every word by heart. This time you can't go in with excuses. Know your lines so well that you simply can't be thrown. And know your character. The director may want to ask you some questions about your preparation before you start. He may ask, "How do you see this character?" Or he may wait until you've done "Take 1" and then ask why you chose to make this character so angry or so aggressive. You better have a good answer for him.

You may even get into a discussion about the script. The director will want to assess how well you related to the material. If you had certain questions while you were preparing and you had to answer them for yourself, you should tell that to the director. Let him know that you approached the material very thoughtfully and answered some unresolved questions because of indications in the script. If you are asked why you chose to do something in a certain way, it's not a good idea to say that you don't know.

By far, the main reason for callbacks is to assess that very elusive thing called chemistry. Chemistry doesn't only mean the attraction between a man and a woman. It could be between two men or two women or a mother and daughter or father and son. It can be any combination of people or it could be a group of people. And unfortunately chemistry is not something you can prepare or practise for. You could do a brilliant audition but just not connect with the other actor in the scene. Also, it's subjective. There are occasions when I might think the chemistry is there and someone else in the room might not, or vice versa. A conspicuous example for me was the movie *Moonstruck* directed by Canadian

Norman Jewison. I never bought the chemistry between Cher and Nicolas Cage. That film was a huge success and Cher won an Academy Award. Obviously I was in the minority, but I would not have cast those two together.

Over the years I have used two different methods to assess chemistry. Sometimes we need to see the rapport of a small group of actors when the piece is an ensemble. In that case, we will ask a number of actors to come in all at the same time and tell them to be prepared to stay for an hour or two, depending on how many people we have invited. Then we'll bring them in to read in groups or pairs and play mix and match. We'll try to get every combination possible so we can assess the matches we like best and eliminate as we go.

The other procedure I have used is to ask the actors to come in to read in prearranged pairs. I will put the pairs together as I see fit.

In both those situations, I will tell each actor who the other actors are who have been invited to the callback. In the case of the prearranged pairs, I will request that they get together in advance and work on the piece before coming to the audition. There will always be plenty of advance notice for an important callback like this, perhaps a week or ten days. We make the whole script available to each of the actors and I will give the names and phone numbers of the agents of the other actors to make it as easy as possible for them to connect.

As I stated earlier, there's no way to prepare or study for chemistry. It's there or it isn't. But the one thing you can do to try to help it along is to take advantage of the opportunity to work with the other actors and rehearse the scene in advance. Whenever I've been involved in this kind of audition, the actors make it their business to get together to work on the scene. If there is one person or one pair that doesn't, believe me, it shows.

If it ever happens that you are asked to come in for this kind of callback and you aren't given the names of any of the other actors, you should ask your agent to call the casting director and request them. We will give them out. Then you should seek out someone who is reading for another part and try to get together to work on the scene even if you weren't asked to. If no one is available, at least you tried. However, if you were specifically asked to join up with a particular actor and that actor is out of town or otherwise engaged, you should again ask your agent to tell the casting director. At that point, I would ask one of the actors who has already been given a partner if he would mind doing it with two partners. No one ever says no. They are thrilled to have a second opportunity to come in.

If you feel that you don't have any chemistry with the person you were paired with, don't worry. Do all that you can, and if we think you were the best actor reading for that part, we will likely have one more audition and ask you to come back another time with someone else who might be more right for you.

There's one other thing we often do to get that chemistry right. If we have already cast one of the leads, we will ask that actor to come in to read with all the actors being considered to play opposite him. He's happy to participate because he will also want the chemistry to be right—both on a personal as well as an artistic level. So if you're called back for one of those auditions, you can try to seek out the person already cast and see if he's prepared to work with you in advance. If you know each other, he may be willing. If you don't or he isn't willing, don't worry. Just do your best. If you're better than everyone else, you'll probably get the part.

So it's simple—just be better than everyone else.

One final comment on chemistry: You may never have thought about it in this way but there has to be a certain chemistry between the actor and the director as well. Call it comfort level or security, but a director will sometimes say that he feels he can work better with one actor over another. He may not be able to articulate why, but he knows that is the case. Often it will influence his decision. That's also chemistry.

debriefing and keeping in touch

DEBRIEFING AND KEEPING IN TOUCH

DEBRIEFING

You nailed it! You came out of the audition and you were convinced that you put it away. As you wait one day, and then two or three days, your confidence starts to flag. Did you really nail it? Maybe the casting director didn't quite see it the way you did. You want to know what the people in the room thought.

Casting Myth #11: "Don't call us, we'll call you." It is true that you can't call the casting director to see if you got the part, but you can get feedback on your audition. Chances are that if the film started shooting yesterday and you still haven't heard from them today, you didn't get it. But that shouldn't stop you from trying to find out how well you did. Discuss it with your agent and see if he or she will call the casting director for you. If he won't, he should have a good reason or maybe you want to rethink your relationship with your agent. Don't call yourself. This is a busy time for a casting director. At this point in the process, I will be preparing for more casting sessions and I will be booking the actors who have already been chosen and negotiating their contracts. So I may be speaking to your agent about other clients and the agent can ask for feedback then.

It's worth noting that feedback can be given to the casting director at this time as well. If you think you blew the audition you should let your agent know. The agent should tell the casting director that this wasn't up to your usual level of ability, so she will continue to call you in for other auditions in the future.

Although you can't do this every time, it is a good idea to get feedback once in a while. I always feel it's a shame that actors can't see the tape of their auditions but they can't. So the next best thing is to ask someone who was in the room what they thought about your performance. Do this only when you get a big audition or if it's one of the first times you have auditioned for a particular casting director. Or perhaps the role asked for a different characterization than the actor usually gives. Sometimes an actor feels he blew it and wants to find out. But never call for feedback if you had just one line to read. Also, if an agent is constantly asking for feedback about a particular client it can suggest the agent is concerned about his client's acting ability.

Whenever I have callbacks I try to call the agents of everyone who came in. The work involved for a callback is a lot more in-depth than for the original audition, so I try to let everyone know how they did. Not every casting director does this, so if you don't get a call after a callback I think you are very justified in asking for feedback. But again, do it through your agent.

Unfortunately, there isn't always a lot I can say. As I pointed out in Chapter 7, there are many occasions when the best audition doesn't get the part, and I can't always admit that. I will always offer that an audition had been excellent if that was the case. Most of the time, however, auditions are okay, only okay. By that I mean they aren't bad, but they don't soar above the rest. It's difficult to comment on an audition like that. I will usually tell the truth: that the audition was fine but someone else was more right for the part, which generally means that someone else did a better audition.

On occasion, I will tell an agent a brutal truth. I might say that the client needs to get some voice training because his voice is thin and annoying. I might say that he had misunderstood the part, and his take on it was off the mark. I may say that the part was a little too demanding for an actor who is at the beginning stages of a career.

Most of the time I find myself saying that we went with someone who was younger or someone older. While that may be true, it also means that your audition didn't stand out above the rest. If your performance was really outstanding, we wouldn't have noticed that your age was off by a few years.

I was present at an audition for series leads where the actors called in were fairly heavy hitters. They had all done big roles and were experienced. The first one to come in was personable and charming when we chatted, but when she started her audition she didn't know her lines—at all. I was surprised because I had gone out of my way to make sure all the actors had the sides four days in advance. This was for a series lead!

After a page and a half, the producer said, "Cut. You're not off book." She laughed and said, "You could tell?" He replied that unfortunately he couldn't assess what she could do with the part. She could have another ten minutes outside if that would help, but he couldn't continue. She said, "I can't learn all this in ten minutes!" Obviously it wasn't nerves. The producer shrugged and said, "Sorry." She left the room shell-shocked.

Imagine my feedback for that one.

So the bottom line: You have to be more than just fine. You have to stand out from the crowd in a positive way. As always, you just have to be better than everyone else.

KEEPING IN TOUCH

Once we have met, most actors have a great desire to keep me informed of every detail of their professional lives. While it's important to keep in touch, you have to be judicious. Don't send me a new résumé every week. Things won't have changed that quickly, either in your life or mine. Here are some appropriate times to get in touch:

- If you have changed your hair length or colour and you have new photos that show it.

- If you are a male and you've changed your facial hair and have new photos that show it.

- If you have just returned from a long gig out of town. Don't send out a notice beforehand to say that you are going out of town because that information is of no use to me. I want to know when you are back and available so I can call you in again.

- If you have changed agents. It's always good for me to know how to find you.

- If you are appearing in a show.

This last one is the most important. If you have a nice role either on stage or on film, you should let as many casting people know about it as possible. If I'm going to the theatre anyway, I might as well watch for you. And if you are appearing in a film or television show, I should look for your performance as well as any others I'm checking. Even if your role isn't very large, if I'm watching anyway it's worth my knowing that you are in the show.

I do appreciate receiving notice of your appearances. What I can't promise is that I'll call you or that I'll be absolutely sure of seeing your show. But I will try.

When you send out these notices, remember the reason you are doing it. You're not doing it to receive a return phone call from me. You just want to let me know about your performance so I can catch it. The best way is to send a fax or use snail mail. If you use e-mail, you risk that I will not print out the message and it will be lost. Also, I do not open attachments from people I don't know. There are too many computer viruses and I won't risk it. You can also leave a message on voice mail or with an assistant. If you get me on the line that's great, but it isn't necessary to get me personally. If you have several things all coming to the screen, either small or large, put them all in one notice. If nothing else, it will be impressive and it will keep your name in the forefront of my mind.

So try to find out the casting director's preference for receiving information. As with agents, some people hate having their e-mail filled with messages from actors, attachments or not. I prefer a fax over e-mail, but I don't want my fax machine tied up receiving photos. So if you plan to include a picture and résumé, use snail mail. In fact, you can never go wrong with snail mail.

One final thought about keeping in touch: use discretion and common sense. You may run into a casting director in a situation that has nothing to do with work. Maybe your children go to the same school and you meet at Parents' Night. Or you might cross paths at the grocery store. I run into a lot of actors at the gym where I work out. It's nice to say hi and chat—but not about the business. Resist the temptation. I can assure you I don't want to hear how you feel you blew your last audition when I'm standing naked in the shower.

*staying busy
when you're not*

CHAPTER TEN

STAYING BUSY WHEN YOU'RE NOT

It's 11;30 in the morning. You're sitting at Second Cup drinking your second latte and reading the Entertainment section of the newspaper when your cellphone rings. This time it's not your agent. In fact, it hasn't been your agent for quite a while, not since your last audition six weeks ago. What to do?

This is probably the most difficult time in an actor's life. The acting muscle has to be exercised just like any other if it's to stay in shape. The trouble is that you need someone to hire you, to give you the opportunity to exercise the muscle on a regular basis.

Or do you?

The reality is that you can do things to keep yourself in shape. And it doesn't have to cost a lot of money. Taking courses and workshops is always valuable, but when your finances are such that it isn't possible, don't despair.

The cheapest way to keep informed about what is going on and who is doing what is to watch television. No matter what criticism is levelled against television, it has no relevance to you. You have to have a healthy respect for all media in which you might have an opportunity to work, and television provides the most opportunity. It's up to you to find out who your competition is and to know what they are doing.

There's lots to watch; even the commercials have value if you are looking at the talent. You should also be familiar with the work of the directors, writers, and producers involved. You'll be more impressive and memorable in auditions if you're conversant with the work of the people you're auditioning for. And it's always nice to be able to compliment someone on their most recent achievement, so make sure you know what their most recent achievement is. Don't be a TV snob. It's part of your homework so watch as much as you can and watch as actively as you can.

Movies are also a valuable form of research. If you would be willing to take a job acting in something, then you can't refuse to pay money to go and see it. So expand your movie choices to include ones you wouldn't ordinarily go to.

Attending theatre may be a little more costly than television or movies, but you can go to pay-what-you-can performances. Fringe festivals are also usually very affordable and very useful. The smaller theatres are well worth the cost. The big mega-productions are more of a problem because of the expense, but they definitely have value. They employ a lot of actors. And don't forget about children's theatre. Many actors get their start there, and it does require slightly different skills.

The more knowledge you have of the Canadian entertainment scene, the better. In the interest of being informed, you should also be reading Canadian literature. Not only is it wonderful, but so much of it gets made into movies.

There are also more active things you can do, such as save the sides from all the auditions you attend and then get together with a group of actors and make a workshop out of it. You may have received some notes at your audition that you can pass along. You can try the other actors' audition pieces and see what happens. If no one is very good at directing or giving criticism, at the very least you will have had an opportunity to work on some new material and practise doing the work involved. If you can videotape the sessions, so much the better. You need to see yourself on camera as much as possible to identify any nervous tics or habits. Only then will you purge them from your acting style.

You can also get together with actors to benefit from each other's experience. If you have had a lot of coaching in voice, and someone else has had more movement training, you can share your knowledge with each other. Refer back to exercises you used in your training and work together teaching each other as much as you can. It's a good way to keep in touch with actors in the same situation as you, and it also keeps those muscles limber.

Obviously you can expand on the workshop idea and get a committed group of people together who would like to workshop a play. Maybe it will lead to someone being able to mount a production in the future or maybe it won't, but you'll learn a lot and definitely keep busy. And that's what you want to do—keep busy. Who knows, you might even learn about producing for theatre and want to pursue it further down the road.

You will certainly be going after any acting work you can get on both professional and student productions, but if you can't get work as an actor for the moment, you might want to consider working on non-paying films in any capacity whatsoever. They are always looking for volunteers. If you offer to get props or sew costumes, your efforts will be hugely appreciated and you'll gain useful experience. It really does help to see who is doing what and how all the jobs fit together. A good actor is the sum total of all his experiences and skills, so this work will always pay dividends. And think of all the contacts you will make.

Sometimes professional productions have enough money to hire a reader for auditions. Or in some cases they might ask an actor to volunteer to be a reader. It's a very interesting and valuable thing to do. First of all, you get to watch a whole day of auditions. Second, you get to hear the discussion that goes on in the room. It can be very revealing to hear what is said on the other side of the door. You also get to practise cold reading a lot of different sides.

A word of warning, however: Being a reader can be a very stressful situation if the director is nervous or if someone is a prima donna. For that reason I won't hire a reader I don't know well. I have to make sure the person I hire is capable of the acting requirements but is also able to cope emotionally and politically. They have to know how much to give and not forget that this is not their own audition but someone else's. They have to know to keep their mouths shut no matter what and not offer opinions. They have to be able to take direction very quickly and they have to, above all, keep their cool. If the director is having a hissy fit, they have to just sit back and let it ride. They also have to be discreet. At one audition the producer was talking about the actors during a break. He turned to the reader and said, "If you repeat any of this, I will have to hunt you down and kill you." I sort of thought he wasn't kidding.

If you have the stomach for it, and have a good relationship with a casting director, you might want to consider doing this. Also, if you're not a union member, let the casting director know if you're willing to do it for free.

Casting Myth #12: You can't work as an extra and expect to be called in to read for a speaking part. There has always been a great deal of discussion surrounding the topic of being an extra, or as they prefer to be called now—background performers. My personal view is that you should do it if you want to. And then do it only as long as you want. When you find it's no longer useful, then stop.

There are casting directors who cast extras and there are casting directors who cast the speaking parts. In some small centres a single person may fulfill both functions, but in every significant film-making centre the functions are divided between two people. Since I don't cast extras, I wouldn't know if you had been working as an extra or not. Nor would I care. In fact, if you had never been on a professional set I would be a little worried about casting you, especially if I had a relatively inexperienced director. So in that regard, including extra work on your résumé would be a plus. At least I would know that you know how daunting it can be when forty or fifty pairs of eyes focus on you after the director says "Action!" If you've never experienced that, then you should. Student films can't prepare you adequately. When there's a crew of two, it's just not the same.

If you can make money and actually work in the field in which you have chosen to spend your life, so much the better. If you can afford to work for what it pays, extra work makes more sense than being a waiter or bartender. There is much that can be learned. You can be a "general extra" in a crowd scene or you can be a "special business extra," where you get to be a nurse or doctor or teacher or police officer in the background of a shot. In those cases you actually have to take direction and learn how to hit your mark and maintain your continuity. And you needn't worry that a director will remember you since it's usually the first assistant director who gives directions to the extras.

At a certain point you may tire of doing general extras but want to continue doing special business. If that's the case, then just accept the ones that you want and refuse the others. But being any kind of extra can eventually become tedious and frustrating. You can also learn the bad habits of the professional extra (complaining about the waiting room or the food, boasting that you could do the part better than the lead actor). So while it does have value, only continue to do it while it's providing you with something you need. When it doesn't serve your purposes any longer, stop doing it.

The same things could be said about doing actor roles when you normally do parts that are much larger. It is misguided to think that will harm your reputation. On the contrary, I will think you are a working actor who wants to keep busy and appear in interesting projects directed by exciting directors.

The name of the game is—keep learning and keep busy.

EPILOGUE

AUDITION STORIES

I was tempted to call this "Audition Horror Stories," but that's not really what they are. Some are anecdotes, some are cautionary tales (reread the section on wardrobe planning in Chapter 3!), but really they are war stories. Some battles you survive and some you don't but you have to go out there prepared to fight. I asked a lot of actors if they had any stories about auditions that they wanted to share and everyone's first reaction was that they certainly did. There were a few universal themes. Most included a rude director who never looked at the actor during the audition. Another was nerves and what happened because of them. But surprisingly there were not that many real "stories" with a beginning, a middle, and an end.

I'm aware that actors often have to put up with a lot in auditions. I heard about directors with accents so thick they couldn't be understood, or directors who had a debilitating stutter. One of them was so bad and it took him so long to get anything out that people had to turn away while he was speaking. One actor actually forgot all his preparation waiting for the stutterer to finish.

Many actresses talked of being asked to come to audition in revealing clothes and then having to pirouette for the camera to each side and then to the back. They thought they'd be able to get through it but were horribly embarrassed when the moment actually arrived. As a casting director I can honestly say that those auditions embarrass me as well. I don't like them. But it can always be worse. I was at one audition where the actress was called back for the fourth time and was asked to be prepared to strip down to a bra and panties. The film had a love scene and the director wanted to make sure that she would be uninhibited enough to do it on the day. Make no mistake: they also wanted to check out her body. We had several male producers show up for that audition who had never attended before. The whole thing just had an unpleasant and nasty feel to it. The actress was very good-natured and appeared to be willing to put up with almost anything. In the end, someone with a bigger "name" got the part.

I was asked on one occasion to check the body of a double we had hired for our marquee actress who wouldn't do nude scenes. The producers suddenly panicked that the double might have a horrible scar or tattoos that wouldn't be appropriate. I have never been asked before or since to conduct such an investigation. I was horrified. I resolved that I would not ask her to take off her panties. I had to draw the line somewhere.

It was a scorching hot summer day. She arrived at my door wearing a skin-tight white sleeveless dress that was ankle-length with a side slit that went almost to the top of her thigh. She was a knockout; all my gawking neighbours thought so too. She chatted as she came in the door and I let her go up the stairs in front of me. As she climbed she was reaching behind her back to undo her zipper. When we arrived at the top of the stairs she let the dress fall to her feet. I needn't have worried about the underwear because she wasn't wearing anything under the dress. She turned around for me, chatting all the while, then pulled up the dress and was on her way. I have never fully recovered.

The moral of these stories is that you should know your own personal boundaries. Decide beforehand what you are comfortable doing and what would mean crossing the line. It doesn't hurt to have a working knowledge of the relevant collective agreement as well. If you have any questions about what is allowed and what isn't, check your agreement or phone a union steward.

Here's a story a very bold and gutsy actress told me: "I went to an audition where the reader was a young man who was wearing very loose shorts on a hot summer day. He sat leaning back in his chair with his legs spread-eagled in front of him. That meant he was also spread-eagled in front of me as I sat in the chair opposite. It seems that everything he owned was hanging down one side of his shorts and was visibly out there for all to see. It was difficult enough to concentrate but to make matters worse, he was playing the part of a woman. Before I started I turned to the director and asked, 'Excuse me, but does Mary Jane have a dick?' That got their attention. The answer of course was no. So I asked if the reader could please be instructed to bring his legs together. He did."

An actress told me about an audition where the director insisted on reading with her. He sat much too close and kept whispering inappropriate things in her ear, which were not in the script. At what point does this become harassment? she thought. Several people told me about auditioning in pairs with perfect strangers where the audition consisted of necking and petting for the camera.

One man in his forties, and self-described as "stout," shared this story:

"I went to an audition where all I was told in advance was that I would be asked to ride a bicycle. When I arrived in the studio a young female casting assistant asked me to mount the bike. She went around behind me, asked me to bend over and then she took a Polaroid shot of my butt. I never got the part or even a callback so I can only wonder what that was all about."

Another man told me about an audition he had with a young boy who was playing his son. The scene was one in which they were supposed to be taking a shower with the father washing the boy. Throughout the whole audition they were being sprayed with water.

And what about unusual direction given to actors? One actress was asked to stomp around the audition room trumpeting like an elephant, with her arms pretending to be the trunk. This was for a toilet-paper commercial. Another actress was called in to read for a young mom. She was given this direction: "Pretend you are a cow hearing thunder for the very first time." Or how about this one: "Play it like a black bitch with a hard-on!"

It certainly helps to retain your sense of humour.

I think it's also interesting to note that we, on the other side of the table, are often witness to the weird and the wacky as well. At one of my recent auditions, a woman who had just given birth a few months earlier came in and her cellphone rang right in the middle of her scene. Ringing cellphones are usually the domain of a producer or a director. In this case, the actress stopped in mid-sentence and said that she had to take the call because it was "a breast-feeding emergency." On another occasion, an actor came in with an earpiece on. He looked like a secret-service agent. He told us that he had a small tape recorder in his pocket with the lines pre-recorded. The scene was very long and he hadn't had time to memorize it. As we worked through the reading, we could all see him listening to his lines on the tape before he responded to his cues. I found it very difficult not to laugh, thinking that if the reader went at a different speed than his tape, the whole thing could have turned out very badly.

We were all amused at an audition where an actor asked if he would have a say in the choice of director.

Every casting director has stories of being attacked. One small woman was almost strangled by a six-foot-five actor. Another time an actor jumped on the table where the producers and director sat, brandishing a real knife. I have been shoved up against the wall and pinned there for the duration. I was present at two different auditions where the actors hadn't taken careful note of which door they entered the room by and then picked the wrong one when it came time to exit. In both cases, the actors chose to stay in the closet rather than face the embarrassment of coming out. I actually understand that. I would probably choose to do the same thing.

One actor told me about his most horrifying moment. When nerves got the better of him during an audition, he forgot his lines. He tried to carry on but just got further and further off course. It occurred to him that he had to find a way out of this hopeless situation. His brain must have jumped a synapse at that moment because he decided the best thing to do would be to disappear altogether. He slid off his stool and crawled on all fours to the door, trying to deliver his lines all the while. He reached up for the knob and escaped without ever having stopped talking. He wasn't the least bit surprised when he didn't receive a callback.

It's a funny thing about nerves and what they can do. I remember one audition where we had Mike Myers come in to read for one of the leads. It was a comedy and he had just returned to Canada from England, where he had recently broken up with his comedy partner. He was looking to start a solo career and this role seemed just the thing. He was so nervous that his audition was awful. He just couldn't do a thing right. Next thing we knew he had auditioned for *Saturday Night Live* in New York and was the toast of television. We'll never know if it was nerves that nixed this one for him or if he is one of those performers who can really only be effective with his own material.

Here's one that takes courage. Although entirely justified, an actress chastised a producer and a director who continued talking during her audition. She stopped her reading, interrupted their chat, and said, "I'll come back when you're finished." She wasn't wrong to do that, but they'll never hire her.

As I pointed out in Chapter 6, it's always risky to follow stage directions in an audition. They can cause you real grief. An actor told me of an audition he was doing with an actress. At one point he grabbed her hand to run as the stage directions instructed. The actress kept pulling back until it seemed they were locked in a tug-of-war. The actor won. He pulled them both right into the camera and knocked it over. She could see what was going to happen and had been trying to save him, but he wasn't getting the message.

Another actor also followed stage directions that told him to run. He was in a small studio and didn't look where he was going. He ended up slamming up against the wall. Ordinarily that wouldn't bruise too much except your ego but in this case the drywall was brand new. The actor actually embedded himself in the wall. He got stuck there and had to be pulled out. While you might make an impression doing this, it's not the kind of impression you want to leave in the room.

Then of course, there are the mistakes one can make with the information given. Here's a personal favourite. An actor got an audition for a New York City-based film as "Random House Guy." He was a method actor and had been watching all the homeless psychiatric patients near his apartment and collected their tics and mannerisms to use at his audition. He worked on his sides and got together an appropriate wardrobe and became the eccentric "house guy" he had been envisioning. All the people in the audition room seemed a little taken aback when they saw him, but no one said anything. They did the slate and he launched into it. In what was described as "a cross between Charles Manson and Rasputin on speed," he delivered the first speech in a menacing array of shouts, mutters, and intense, almost obsessive pacing as he spoke to the problems he was having with "Bob" and what to do about them. The reader was so shocked that he just froze in wonder, without delivering any lines. Only then did it dawn on our hero that he wasn't actually a random "House Guy" but was supposed to be an editor at Random House Publishing. He ad libbed a few lines about deadlines and left. He was too embarrassed to venture out of his home for two days.

Then there is the story of the young actor who was going to the States for a very important audition. He had on a bite plate with two false teeth, which he was wearing while he awaited the dental appointments that would permanently place those teeth in his mouth. On the plane he got horribly sick. His bite plate ended up in the airsick bag. Without his two "eye teeth" and sporting a pronounced lisp, he saw no reason at all to show up for the audition so he cancelled. The moral of this story is to carry a spare at all times—whether bite plate or glasses or any other necessity.

Here are a couple of stories about feedback. I'm sure the casting directors who made these comments would be horrified to realize what they said or what could be taken from what they said. A very beautiful young actress with a great body was asking the casting director how she did and he said, "Your audition was good, but you have to lose twenty pounds." In another case, a stunning woman, tall and slim, asked a casting director why she hadn't been brought in to audition for a certain role. The casting director responded, "Well, my dear, 'so-and-so' got the part and she's beautiful!"

My final story stands alone. Perhaps this more than anything else gives an insight into the fact that you can never really tell what is actually going on in the room. I had been casting the lead in a new television series for about five months when we were very close to making a decision. The producers and the director wanted one more session just to make sure that we hadn't overlooked anyone in our search. The day was long—five hours—and with only one character being auditioned, we grew extremely tired of hearing the same words over and over and over again, especially since we had been hearing them on and off for five months. At about the three-hour mark, the executive producer who had written the script said that he would like to be the reader for the next audition, just to change the dynamic in the room. I vacated my chair and gave it to him. Then I brought in the next actor. All started well enough, but after a few lines of dialogue the producer started to sweat. Eventually his white shirt was soaked through. When he took off his glasses to wipe his forehead he made a spray of drops. When the audition finally ended and the actor left the room, the producer turned to look at us and was so shocked at how nervous he had been that he just said, "What the hell was that about?" We convulsed into uncontrollable laughter that had nothing at all to do with the actor or the very decent audition he had given us.

I was about to take back my chair when the line producer said that he now wanted a turn. When the actor came in, things got even worse. This producer couldn't make it through the first page of the script without losing it and having to stop tape because he was laughing so hard. I should stress that this was not a comedic scene. He composed himself and managed to hold it together long enough to get through the audition. Again, when the actor left the room, we burst out laughing. We took a real break and got back on track. I brought in the next actor and with me reading things went smoothly. When he was done the executive producer complimented the actor on the very good job he had done and the actor responded, "Well, thank you very much, but I just wish I could have been as funny as the last two guys!"

I've included that story for two reasons. First, it is true that you can't tell what is going on in the room so you have to continue to believe that you are the best person for the role and that the audition you gave is the best audition they will see—no matter what. But I think that story is important for another reason. When I am asked to give casting seminars to producers and directors, I always try to include a few minutes where I get them to do mock auditions for me. I want them to experience just a tiny bit of what you have to experience all the time. Even though they are in a safe environment with friends and colleagues, they get terrified. And what's more, they are surprised by just how terrified they become. I think that's great. I wish I could get all producers and directors to experience what actors go through at every audition. It would certainly make them more understanding when they are behind the table the next time.

Okay, you've done enough procrastinating. Now it's time to get to work. Even though you won't win every time, you have to get out there believing in yourself and prepared to do battle. Hopefully, soon, when you've done the best you can, and all the stars are aligned in the right way, you'll be sitting at Second Cup when your cellphone rings the day after an audition. You'll answer and this time you'll hear your agent roaring at you,

"You got the part!"